simplestyle

creating relaxed interiors in the contemporary home

Julia Bird

text by Bridget Bodoano photography by Hotze Eisma

Publishing Director: Anne Furniss
Art Director: Mary Evans
Project Editors: Nicki Marshall & Lisa Dyer
Designer: Sue Storey
Illustrator: Bridget Bodoano
Production: Sarah Tucker

First published in 2001 by Quadrille Publishing Ltd, Alhambra House,
27-31 Charing Cross Road, London WC2H 0LS

Cataloguing in Publication Data: a record for this book is available from the
British Library.

ISBN 1 902757 65 3

Printed in Singapore

Contents

Part One

Elements
of simple

the simple approach

Simplicity is the essence of contemporary interior style. Creating a blank canvas on which to arrange essential possessions and inject personal touches is the first step towards a calmer, more composed ambience in which to enjoy your home. A simple style approach is about looking at new ways to use space and colour, choosing materials and furnishings and addressing the challenges of storage to design a look that is unfussy, comfortable, easy to live in and reflects your own individuality.

gold and silver simple glass line and figure organic texture brick and metal

Space is an important element, whether you add space by removing walls for open-plan living or simply use a pale colour to create an illusion of space. Much of the style and feel of an interior relates to the materials and surfaces used throughout. The mellow qualities of existing or reclaimed materials add character. New materials are crisper and smoother, and will sharpen and modernize a setting. Steel and glass add definition, while natural stone and wood bring harmony through colour and texture.

crisp linen white and neutral ordered displays blue and white reflective metals

White and neutral colours enhance the feeling of space, bring light and freshness to a room and provide an unobtrusive backdrop for furnishings. Bolder colours inject life, accent and contrast. Functional, practical and hard-working pieces of furniture offer a simple honesty. Colours, surfaces, textiles and shapes can be chosen to blend into the surroundings or to stand out as features. Combining a mix of styles will help to create an original look. Incorporating storage will assist in the

painterly palettes soft and hard-edged fresh florals antique and modern

creation of a clutter-free, streamlined environment and ensure that it remains so. Shelving provides the opportunity to display favourite belongings or collections or to highlight the beauty of a simple arrangement, such as a stack of white china or a row of books. The simple approach is not a fixed style; it encompasses a wide variety of looks, from the strict discipline of white-on-white to the joyous celebration of raw materials. It allows you to put together a style which is both personal and unique.

pattern and plain rough-hewn stone light and space natural wood clean and clear

Right **The open-plan layout of this maisonette in a former artist's studio ensures the character of the building is retained and allows an abundance of light to penetrate into every area. Structural pillars and beams have been painted white to simplify the space. The first floor houses the living and kitchen areas, while the bedroom and office are on the ground floor.**

space

A desire for more space and light has become an important aspect of contemporary interior design, influencing the way we use and allocate space. The appeal of loft living and the allure of minimalism lies in large, calm spaces and pared-down simplicity, which is a perfect antidote to the fast pace of busy lives. A demand for flexible interiors that can be adapted to accommodate changing lifestyles and needs has also led to a less defined use of rooms. More general living areas have been opened up, where cooking, eating, relaxing and even working can all take place within a larger and more sociable space.

Not everyone has the luxury of large amounts of space, but creating a spacious feel in even the tiniest apartment is possible by employing imagination and disciplined control. A simple style approach is as much about achieving a feeling or an illusion of space as it is about maximizing space and this can be achieved by careful and considered use of colour and materials, together with a paring-down of furniture and other possessions.

A collection of rooms, each with a different function and decorating scheme, can be transformed into a single cohesive space by painting the walls and paintwork a similar colour and carrying the same floor surface throughout. Glossy surfaces are more reflective and make a room seem bigger, while painting ceilings in a lighter colour than the walls makes them appear higher. Bare floors and walls and a restrained use of furnishings enhance a spacious feel.

Central heating and more sociable ways of living reduce the need for doors between rooms. Open doorways allow light, and the eye, to travel unimpeded throughout the space. Simply removing doors will make a difference, but enlarging a doorway, by widening it or making it floor-to-ceiling height, can make a

Above **Open metal-frame
kitchen fittings and the
metal stair rail are entirely
in keeping with the
commercial origins of the
building, as is the wall of
cupboards used to divide
the kitchen and sitting
areas. The use of white,
pale grey and reflective
metals keeps this relatively
small home spacious,
and the skylight above
allows even more light to
enter the space.**

space   13

Left **An otherwise dark narrow staircase has been transformed into a sculptural feature with an open, stepped side. Not only does the design allow light to enter, but it also highlights the beauty of the oak stairs, which link to the floors and skirting boards.**

radical change, and this is easier and less drastic than removing a wall. Raising the height of doorways also gives the illusion of higher ceilings. Freeing up the circulation routes encourages better use of the space as a whole, as rooms that may have been under-used become more accessible.

The desire to maintain the full impact of high ceilings and large areas of floor and windows has led to open-plan living. Structural work, including knocking down walls, building extensions and opening up roof spaces, creates more space. Opening up the whole of one floor can be dramatic and successful. You will almost certainly acquire a better-lit environment – windows will expose the space to more light during the day, illuminating areas that were previously dark or perhaps never received direct sunlight. Glazed glass roofs or skylights can be installed, which allow light into the centre of a home or brighten dark hallways. Opening up narrow, poorly lit

Right **The doorway to this bedroom has been enlarged, adding a sense of space and height, and giving a more contemporary and unexpected feel. When left open, the custom-built panelled door allows light from both sides to flood into the room.**

areas, such as hallways and staircases, has an immediate effect. Open stairs allow light from above to penetrate to lower floors, or vice versa. Remember to provide areas for storage when reconstructing a space. Dark areas can house utility equipment, shower cubicles or bathrooms, where natural light is not so necessary.

The demand for housing in cities has resulted in the conversion of redundant warehouses, factories and offices into loft spaces. Usually bought as a shell, they offer a unique opportunity to radically alter the conventional layout of a home. Instead of the old wood and rough stonework seen in some country properties, original materials, such as brick, concrete, raw wood, metal and cast iron, have been left in place in lofts and are much admired for their industrial references. Mezzanine levels, sleeping platforms and open walkways are all ways of retaining the character and open aspect of warehouse buildings and a desire to emulate this

Right **Here, a warm ambience is derived from the colours of the exposed brickwork and raw wood of the staircase and original floorboards. Smoother, paler wood, used for the table and benches, adds a calmer, more sophisticated feel. A full-height floating partition wall, adorned by a picture, separates a dining space from the kitchen area beyond.**

Left **The charm and character of a small stone barn has been retained by leaving the beams and roof timbers exposed and keeping the built-in wall around the sleeping area as low as possible. Blue paintwork, seen here on the bed surround, has been used throughout all areas of the home to provide continuity. Its cool colour enhances the feeling of space and adds a restful air.**

Above **To avoid any loss of space, the whole of this industrial interior has been opened up. An old salvaged staircase, with its warm, raw wood, has been placed in the centre of the ground floor to act as a room divider between the living and dining areas.**

urban style has had a significant influence on how space is defined and used in even the most traditional of homes. In converted barns and country properties, traditional steep roofs and old beams and trusses may be left exposed and galleried sleeping areas can take the place of traditional bedrooms to maximize space. Painting low, beamed ceilings white also increases the feeling of space.

Keep in mind that it is not always possible, desirable or wise to open up large areas of a house or flat, particularly if the property is rented, the structure unsuitable, changes are too costly or it simply does not suit a particular lifestyle. Open-plan living may work well for individuals or couples, but family life usually benefits from some closed-off areas.

Arranging furniture and kitchen fittings or delineating specific areas often requires some form of division. Solutions include installing floating walls or using a large cupboard or shelf as a dividing unit. Short, central partition walls

define areas without cutting them off and provide a surface for fixtures and fittings, as necessary in a kitchen, or for a piece of furniture or a picture. A three-quarters-height wall allows light to enter and provides a place to conceal necessities. For example, a range of kitchen fittings or an office may be sited in a convenient and discreet position behind a wall, rather than placed conventionally along an outside wall where it may interrupt continuity of line. Kitchens and bathrooms, often arranged in the centre of a home, can be designed within a sculptural 'pod' or island to enhance the space. Another way to ensure the maximum amount of light and keep spaciousness as the focus is to place all furniture and fittings in the centre of a space, leaving the outside edges clear.

Sliding walls, screens and tall doors enable areas to be closed off into smaller spaces for privacy or a change of function. Tall glass doors can be used to block off areas but keep light flowing through and provide sound insulation.

Right **A low, modern daybed on a slender metal frame and a simple suede-covered cube emphasize the high ceilings and generous proportions of this pared-down minimal interior. A loose-fitting, pale linen cover, piles of cushions and a bare brick fireplace add touches of comfort.**

Floor-to-ceiling doors, either pivoting, sliding or folding, become part of the structure.

Although cooking, eating, entertaining and relaxing often take place within a single large space, bedrooms are still considered a haven of peace and privacy. Most people opt for smaller sleeping areas in favour of more space for day-time activities. As a result, bedrooms can be kept quite small or tucked into roof voids. Storing clothes and personal belongings out of sight in a dressing room, bathroom or walk-in or built-in wardrobe ensures a calm, restful and spacious atmosphere. A bed may be positioned in the centre of the room, against a partition or floating wall, with space all round the edges.

Working from home is becoming increasingly common and allocating space for work depends on how you work, how much space you need and who else shares your home. A dedicated home office keeps all work-related matters and materials away from other aspects of life, but if space is scarce, integrate a workstation into a storage system (see page 45) or incorporate it into a partition wall. Opening up space may also create an opportunity to place a workspace in a previously unused area. Alternatively, a large, uncluttered living space can be conducive to work, in which case it is sensible to use it during the day and convert it back to a sitting room when work is finished for the day.

Right **A floating wall, complete with the same classical detailing as the rest of the room, allows a bed to be placed away from the outside walls, thus dividing the space in an interesting and unexpected way and opening up a view to the garden. Both dramatic visual impact and some privacy is provided.**

Sometimes a space is so beautiful in its own right that it seems a pity to put anything in it. Bare walls and floors and uncovered windows look stunning, especially if the architectural detailing is of high quality. Wherever possible, keep an interior bare and, for minimal impact, use simple, straight-edged furnishings in neutral tones or colours to match the walls. Long, low furniture emphasizes the elegant proportions of a large space and makes a smaller room appear bigger. However seductive the idea of empty space may be, don't compromise on comfort and normal life to keep it that way. Space, whether real or illusionary, should be stimulating as well as restful, and lived in, not just admired.

materials

Above **The contrasts of
rough-hewn stone with a
modern tap and sleek
stainless steel fitted behind
an old enamelled sink
demonstrate the variety of
styles and materials that
can be used in kitchens.
A traditional wooden
draining board looks warm
and familiar, while a
concrete work surface is
easy to clean, smooth and
distinctly modern.**

The use and suitability of materials are often linked to the style of a property. Stone flagstones and rough wooden beams in country houses have immense charm and character, while polished wood and panelled walls in period homes contribute to a more sophisticated ambience. Warmer materials benefit from being allowed to stand out against light-coloured walls and opened-up spaces.

Industrial buildings and warehouses have a wonderful textural patina of brick, raw solid wood and dull steel. A palette of exposed brickwork, untreated wood, cast iron and unpolished metal has lots of character but also a surprising amount of warmth. The terracottas and soft greys of brick harmonize beautifully with the warm tones of thick oak planks and matt surfaces of iron and steel. Adding sharper and

brighter elements, such as stainless steel and glass, gives a space a cleaner, lighter feel. Conversions of newer commercial properties focus on concrete, smooth wood, shiny steel and galvanized metal, while the new institutional style features rubber and terrazzo flooring, painted metal and laminates. Architecturally designed homes often contain glass, stainless steel, acrylics, plywood and veneers. Many traditional materials are now being developed to make them cheaper and easier to use. More precise manufacturing techniques give a sharper look that is well suited to modern living.

If you have an old property with original materials in good condition, and you like them, build a palette of complementary or contrasting materials around them. Remember, there are no rules: it is not imperative to retain original

Left **A varied, yet harmonious collection of materials and styles are evident in this kitchen, including an old-fashioned porcelain sink set in a modern stainless-steel frame and an efficient restaurant-style cooker. Practical wall tiles in pale beige complement the terrazzo worktop and work well with the wooden floor and furniture. Mixing light and dark surface tones gives depth and balance to the room.**

Right **A contemporary concrete sink, reminiscent of the old-fashioned stone variety, is integrated here into a worktop with a satin-finish modern tap. The functional look is completed with plain white splashback tiles and painted cupboard doors, which allow the concrete surface to stand out.**

materials, nor is it necessary to restrict yourself to traditional or historically accurate ones when considering changes. Existing surfaces can be stripped out and replaced. Although some, such as original flags, may be difficult to remove, others, like wooden flooring, can often be floated on top. Mixing new and old gives a more modern feel and allows individuality. For example, easy-to-clean surfaces work well in older properties, a salvaged floor may be installed in a modern style of home and introducing materials associated with industrial spaces into a conventional home creates a contemporary look.

The impact of a chosen material depends on how it is used and in what quantity. Flooring is likely to be the largest area to be covered and therefore has the greatest influence on the look and feel of an interior (see pages 184–9). Blending floors with the walls and structure provides a simple, uniform backdrop. A floor becomes a dramatic and dominant feature when

it is very dark, patterned or boldly coloured. This can work well in an extremely pared-down environment, where a dark floor anchors the space, but can also give cosiness in smaller rooms, such as bedrooms.

Polished or painted concrete flooring is new and industrial-looking. When used with modern furniture it looks sophisticated, but it can also seem functional and practical in a family kitchen. Concrete adds an edge to a more contemporary home – even if furniture and fittings are classical, concrete can make the interior feel new.

Stone is now widely used for flooring, as it has the right qualities for a simpler look. It is also suitable for worktops and makes unusual – and stunning – sinks and basins. Pale, subtle limestones and soft grey slates are frequently used, with the occasional piece of dark granite or marble for contrast. Composite materials and ceramic and terrazzo tiles combine machine-made precision, clean edges and more regular

Above **Woods in different finishes work well together as they have a natural affinity. Here the richness of the old polished chairs and a table with a patinated top contrasts nicely with the duller, paler finish of reclaimed floorboards.**

Right **Wooden planks, used for the kitchen units and a panelled wall, have a natural and characterful finish that is tempered by the streamlined design of the units and the presence of modern stainless-steel appliances and a polished concrete floor. Elsewhere, white walls and paintwork maintain a light feel.**

patterning with the subtle colours of the stone and clay from which they mostly derive. Mosaic tiles add texture and a subtle pattern to a simple interior. Handmade and hand-glazed Moroccan versions in variegated colours have individuality and an artistic feel (see page 32). Butting tiles closely together so only a little grouting is seen gives a more sophisticated look.

Wood is remarkably versatile and available in many guises, from the magnificence of rich, dark, swirly grained varieties to the restrained elegance of pale, subtly marked types. With its natural flexibility, which is kinder to feet, wood makes ideal flooring and is quieter and warmer than rigid stone or concrete. Old wooden floors have a highly prized, mellow quality. Wood is excellent for older properties as it blends in with the surroundings and always looks right, but it can also bring character and warmth to new homes. Oak block is solid and substantial and wide polished planks add a glow to any interior.

Above **Slate tiles make an ideal flooring material in this country barn conversion, as they complement both the style of the building and a lifestyle that involves muddy boots. The addition of a capacious wooden cupboard is a practical and attractive storage solution.**

Right **Enormous original stone flagstones indicate the age and history of a farmhouse. Their worn, irregular surface contains an extraordinary mélange of greys. Combined with white paint, coir-fitted stairs and blue furnishings, they look warm, as well as simple.**

Right Simple wooden stairs and a metal handrail are in tune with the rest of this former artist's studio. The mosaic floor, inherited with the space, has been retained. Its texture and sea blue colour are enhanced by a simple geometric pattern picked out in a lighter blue.

Far right **A white-painted floor unites the structural elements of this elegantly proportioned house so that the space and architectural detailing take precedence over the materials. Cornices and mouldings provide a subtle hint of decoration when white and maintain an historical reference.**

New wooden floors combine a smooth surface and pristine condition with the natural characteristics of wood and will liven up any space. A traditionally laid floor in solid wood is a worthwhile investment, but laminated floors are less expensive. Because all wood comes from essentially the same source, even distinctly different varieties naturally harmonize. Mixing them produces a warm medley of tones and textures. Not all wood is attractive enough or of sufficient quality to be left bare, but painting floors, along with walls and any fitted furniture, in a single colour or subtle tones of the same shade creates a cohesive background.

Carpeting and flooring materials consisting of natural fibres work well in a neutral environment and will run seamlessly throughout large spaces. Sisal, sea grass and coir all add warmth and texture. Although of a similar quality to wood, they are a softer-looking alternative, while carpeting is quiet and comfortable underfoot.

Metal plays a more dominant role in interiors than ever before. Stainless steel is particularly popular, especially in kitchens where it is now seen as worktops, splashbacks, cupboards and appliances. It is practical and favoured for its cool, clean, industrial look. Galvanized metal has a less perfect finish than stainless steel, but weathers beautifully, developing a depth of dull tone and withstands a lot of wear and tear. It gives an industrial feel to a home and can be used for staircases and balustrading, shelving and kitchen units. Zinc has a smooth surface with a depth of greeny grey colouring that develops a subtle, more matt patina with age. It can be wrapped around worktops and tables to provide a functional surface.

Glass is an important component of modern-day architecture, where large glass panels are used structurally to give a light, elegant feel. Within domestic interiors it has a similar effect. Glass doors and walls divide areas with minimum

Left **Stunningly simple, this washbasin has been fashioned out of a single slender limestone slab. A tap runs directly out of the wall, allowing the whole unit to meld seamlessly into the surroundings. The look is an intriguing mix of austerity and sophistication.**

impact and translucent, etched glass filters the light beautifully. It looks fresh and modern and works equally well in all styles of property. Glass can make an older house look startlingly up-to-date and can transform a featureless apartment into a smart, sophisticated environment. Wired safety glass has just the right functional look for contemporary interiors influenced by the loft or industrial style and it works well with metal, too.

Plastics have the advantage of a consistently even quality, finish and colour and may be moulded and formed into curvaceous or sharp-edged shapes. They can be obtained in bright dense colours or soft translucent shades. Their use is mostly confined to furniture and accessories, but sheet plastics are also used for splashbacks, screening and even blinds.

Wallpaper can create a feature in a room. Keeping the style, colour or material similar to the rest of the contents in an interior ensures that the overall effect is simple. The newest ranges

combine large-scale patterns with subtle colourings and look effective when they decorate just one wall. Imaginative use can also be made of individual sheets of unusual papers or lengths of fabric. Avoid wallpaper in areas of heavy wear as it cannot be cleaned easily; place it above a dado rail or in an under-used room, such as a guest bedroom, where it will stay clean.

When choosing a surface, pay particular attention to its physical properties. For example, sisal is coarse-textured and will feel rough on bare feet; a gleaming stainless-steel table may look beautiful, but it can be cold and noisy when used. Avoid monotony by combining tones and textures. For example, using only rough and rustic materials can look heavy, so mix in smoother, more refined finishes to lighten and simplify the effect. Similarly, rather than using one colour and finish, try to achieve a more subtle and harmonious feel with different textures and lighter and darker tones.

Above **These three examples demonstrate the diversity of natural materials. The rugged characteristics of stone are seen on a zinc-topped shelf, while fibrous Japanese handmade papers hung on the wall resemble panelling. Irregular, hand-thrown, glazed ceramic bowls contrast with a dramatically dark and smoothly polished granite surface.**

colour

Colour plays an important role in creating a look, style or mood and can be used to unify, highlight, dramatize and, when necessary, to hide or disguise. Colour has the power to change the atmosphere and character of a home. Sometimes a fresh coat of paint is all that is required, but equally the addition of something as simple as a cushion or a throw brings a room to life or makes it more restful. Recognizing that colour exists in the most subtle off-white as well as in bold red makes creating a palette for your interior more interesting and satisfying.

With the simple approach, colour is most often used to create a composed, discreet background and maintain a feeling of space, but it can also develop and enhance an existing colour theme or announce a change of setting. Cool colours, such as blues and greens, give a sense of space and a restful, tranquil feel, making them particularly effective choices for bedrooms and bathrooms. The more white a colour includes, the more reflective it will be and the greater the feeling of space. Warm colours tend to draw a space inward, making it seem

Above left **A set of modern chairs in bright pink and red brings a jolly splash of colour to this country kitchen. Striped red, orange, pink and beige curtains link to the chairs and floor tones, while a white vinyl tablecloth adds informality and increases the effect of the colours.**

Left Cushions are the only colour present in an all-white environment. Made from recycled scarves in orange printed silks and backed with a dark brown tweed, they stand out dramatically against minimal surroundings and introduce texture, pattern and personality.

Right In such a pared-down setting, a pair of splendid retro-style chairs with metal frames can be appreciated for their ingenuous, wonderfully curving design, as well as for the clear purity of colour and the smooth texture of their fitted upholstered covers.

Above **The grey of the paint-washed floor is present in both the subdued colouring of the damask upholstered chair and the muted pattern of the woven throw. In a deceptively simple way, the autumnal colours of the throw and the upholstery harmonize well together.**

Left **Old brown leather has a particularly mellow quality, beautifully complemented here with a soft brown velvet seat. These hues, echoed in the bold modern print of a single, large cushion, stand out wonderfully against the white background.**

Above **A restrained palette of neutral colours is derived from the warm pale grey paint of the panelled wall and box seat, combined with the glowing wood of the tabletop and the well-worn paintwork of the wooden chairs.**

more cosy. White is perhaps the ultimate simple colour. It looks clean and fresh, reflects maximum light and provides a perfect antidote to a busy lifestyle. When used for walls and floors, it transforms an interior into a large blank canvas on which a palette of colours, materials and objects can be arranged.

Many different interpretations of white are available in paint colours, materials and furnishings (see also pages 182–3 and 190–1). Brilliant white is tinged with blue and looks wonderfully bright, pristine and cool, but is also hard and unforgiving and will highlight any imperfections. Brilliant white paint works best in homes with lots of light and good architectural detailing. Glossy white, painted on woodwork, is highly reflective and can give an illusion of space in smaller homes.

Some white paints are based on historic colours, which have been produced from natural and often indigenous materials and pigments.

They have a wonderful authenticity, which can evoke an aura of age in even the newest property. Natural or organic paints include beautiful chalky whites that have a 'rounded' rather than a stark quality. Hints of the whole spectrum have been added to white to create different shades and moods. Cream, white tinged with yellow, and soft beige, with dashes of brown or green added to white, are useful natural colours. Some are inspired by elements outdoors, such as stone or straw.

A white shell is the easiest starting point for creating a blank canvas, though warmer neutral hues are also good choices. While a room may contain only white-painted surfaces and white objects, the range of colours within those whites can nevertheless form a surprisingly wide palette, ranging from the yellowy whites of old painted wood, through grey tones of marble and warm beiges of stone, to the clean whites of new paint or bleached cotton.

Right **Blue gives a tranquil feel to rooms. Using a strong blue on the walls, paintwork and bath panel makes a white bath, basin and fittings appear clean and fresh. The blue woodwork and slate floor run throughout the house, providing continuity. The only other colour present is the pale golden brown of wood, which reinforces the use of wood in the room.**

Palettes based on nature and natural materials offer myriad possibilities. The range of colours within natural substances is enormous and the number of colours, shades and tones present in even one small piece of wood or stone is enough to suggest a whole colour scheme. Shades can vary from the richness of dark wood and the speckled grey of granite, to the ecru of natural linen and the pale subtlety of limestones. Pale neutrals, including buffs, beiges and greys, provide a harmonious ambience when mixed with white, but several different neutrals used together also produce a lively mélange of colour that can be further highlighted with the use of textured materials (see pages 20–7).

Most natural materials have an inherent warmth. Raw metal is dark and dull and only when polished will it attain a cooler look. Similarly linens and cottons in their natural state have a brown or yellow tinge that is cooled and freshened with bleach or sunlight. Worn textiles, wood and stone have a special colour quality that is difficult to reproduce artificially and therefore old

furniture, linens and other artefacts are highly prized. Using different tones or shades of the same colour throughout the whole of an interior maintains continuity and simplicity, but prevents a space from looking too bland or clinical.

However, it is not essential to keep slavishly to a restrained palette. Natural colours also include a mix of deeper and stronger hues, as well as clear brights. Think of the variety of rich reds, oranges and greens of vegetables and fruit, or the elusive blues and aquas of sky and sea. These can provide useful accents or saturations of a tone against a white or neutral background. Deeper and stronger colours add life and can change or enhance the character or mood of a room or a whole house, but achieve more impact when used as accents or flashes of colour.

The addition of bright colours in the form of cushions, throws or bedlinens will cheer up a neutral environment. Brightly coloured chairs or accessories lift a mostly white space, drawing attention to the colour but also to the shape or special characteristics of an object. A bold

Above **Rather than attempting to lighten the effect of richly coloured Moroccan tiles, dense blue and green paint emphasize the liveliness and wealth of different tones and shades of colour in the ceramic glazes. The white sink and stainless-steel cooker sharpen the look and ensure a modern feel.**

Left **The depth of colour
and reflective quality in
these glazed tiles and
traditional ceramics has a
painterly feel. Using both
blue and green, which share
the same intensity of colour,
is bold and brave. However,
the disciplined palette and
lack of distractions keep
the arrangement simple as
well as dramatic.**

Above **Incorporating books into a colour scheme is visually effective and disciplined. Books fall easily into colour groups and the whole effect is one of designed organization.**

pattern on a single cushion in a white space can be a focal point, where it will stand out despite its relatively small presence. Build a scheme for the whole interior around a well-loved object, favourite painting or piece of furniture. While the colour of all the objects in a room will have an effect on the surroundings, a white background allows frequent changes of colour.

A bold use of colour on walls or furnishings can be kept simple by limiting the number of colours used. Using a single colour throughout, with variations in shade, tone, intensity, finish, texture and material, can be dramatic if the colour is warm, but also restful and subtle when softer or cooler hues are used. A stronger, more saturated version of the wall or floor colour

painted on furniture in the room looks effective. Moroccan tiles, with their myriad variations of intense greeny blues and turquoise, provide a magnificent basis on which to build a colour scheme. Isolating them against a light colour may make them seem brash and harsh, but applying them within areas of flat colour in complementary tones will emphasize them while still keeping them controlled.

A traditionally feminine scheme, with soft chalky colours and a scattering of floral prints, becomes simpler when the prints are monochrome and match the colour of the walls, and any other fabrics are in the same solid colour. Dark or dense colours will draw a room in – an alternative option is to use these colours to

emphasize the cosiness of a small room. Painting a bold colour on just one wall of an otherwise monochrome interior provides contrast and drama and may also act as a link to other, smaller amounts of the same colour used elsewhere in the space.

Colour not only unifies a space, but also a disparate group of objects. It can also be used to disguise less-than-perfect features and makes large objects look less obtrusive by blending them into the background. A group of wooden chairs of different styles becomes a uniform set when painted the same colour and a set of matching, but dull chairs can be enlivened by painting them in varying shades of one colour. This treatment works particularly well with fabrics,

where a collection of upholstery or loose covers can be coordinated in a similar materials.

Organizing accessories and necessities by colour helps to create a cohesive environment. Magazines often have obligingly consistent white spines and can be placed in orderly piles. Books can be divided into colour groups to provide a complaisant but surprising collection, or arrange glassware or china by colour for impact.

Have confidence with colours and allow them to reflect your personality. Bright, exuberant, extrovert colours can be used in large, well-lit rooms. Painting is the easiest way to experiment with colour, as walls, floors and furniture can easily be painted over again if a colour palette or scheme doesn't work out as planned.

furnishings

Simple style is not about perfection or minimalism, but about creating an effortless, uncomplicated and easy, lived-in look. Homes that reflect the personality and occasional quirkiness of their owners are preferable to an over-considered or self-conscious style, or one that conforms rigidly to furnishings from the same era. Pieces should be simple and functional. Furnishings are not only practical and functional, but are also an important component of the overall interior, where they can add character and focus or blend into the background. While clean lines and simplicity contribute to an uncluttered look, a pared-down environment also provides the ideal backdrop for a piece that is a little more decorative, unusual, larger or more flamboyant.

Changes in living and working patterns have led to a different approach to how we choose and arrange our furnishings. In order to create a calmer, less cluttered environment, furnishings should work as an edited collection rather than a random selection. Leaving space around a piece

gives it more visual impact. Beautiful, well-designed, good-quality or characterful pieces will be shown to best advantage and less distinctive items can still work well by virtue of their obvious usefulness or anonymity.

More space and less furniture changes the perception of scale and proportion of an interior – items previously thought too large may look and fit perfectly into a more spacious setting. Clearing away superfluous items, such as fussy upholstered chairs or side tables, will make room for a large piece, such as a sofa, which can then become the central feature of a room. When choosing furniture, eschew the over-stuffed and over-blown in favour of smarter shapes and tactile fabrics. Consider whether a piece is good enough to create a focus or whether it should be treated or covered in some way to blend more unobtrusively (see page 211). Introduce your most well-loved piece into an interior first and then add other furnishings, examining how they relate and work with each other. This method

Above left **In a wonderful mix of styles, a colourful piece of ethnic fabric is placed casually over the back of a modern sofa, covered in an antique monogrammed linen sheet.**

Above right **The elegant long curves and richly worn leather of an old armchair become a focal point in a serene interior.**

Above **Both of these chairs are cleaned and restored junk-shop finds. Rather than treating them in the same way, each has been given a separate identity through different fabric choices and methods of covering.**

Left **Undeniably luxurious, this generously sized chaise longue is perfectly complemented and enhanced by a sheepskin cushion. The soft taupe of the cushion blends beautifully with the linen sofa cover and pale grey background wall.**

Right **The exuberant style of the custom-designed ironworked chairs and matching table base adds curves to the rather austere surroundings. Moroccan tiles, embedded into the tabletop, are also used elsewhere in the interior (see page 32). Here the tiles are set within a wide greeny grey border to form a heat-resistant surface for hot drinks and plates.**

Left **The geometric simplicity of the chairs, table and lamp is emphasized by their whiteness. Together with the cool blue of the mosaic floor, they allow the tall glass-fronted bookcase to dominate. Control of this eclectic mix of furniture is achieved by keeping functional pieces white and streamlined, which creates a strong working environment in contrast to the warm, lived-in feel of the cupboard.**

Above **Built-in, high-back seating in a dining area gives a clean functional look while also dividing and delineating the space. Painted in a similar colour to that of the walls, the units become part of the structure. The free-standing oak table has been custom-made to fit into the unit and links with the oak cabinets in the kitchen (not shown).**

also gives you an idea of how to use the space and what the circulation routes will be.

With their easy comfort and open look, daybeds are an alternative to sofas. They look inviting and accessible when positioned in the centre of the room and can vary from the sleek and low to the generously upholstered. Large sofa units, with sections that can be arranged to suit the space, are versatile, make good use of corners and are useful in small rooms.

Old upholstered chairs are comforting and comfortable. Traditional versions look fresher in a modern environment, but they can be easily updated with loosely fitting covers to work anywhere (see page 213). Covers enable a sofa or chair to be incorporated into a colour scheme, either as a contrast or to blend in, and they can be used to disguise a less-than-perfect shape or condition. Casual-fit loose covers and tie-on

slipcovers are easy to remove for laundering and look suitably simple. A throw or length of patterned fabric will disguise an unattractive piece. Tailored or fitted covers suit modern furniture or period styles and can emphasize the shape of a handsome piece. Greys and dark browns are practical choices since they won't show the dirt, which is particularly useful for upholstery that cannot be removed.

Various upholstery fabrics, from the smooth matt finish of felted wool to the crisp textures of natural linen, create different looks. Felted wools look beautiful and tactile, but require special laundering. Utilitarian cottons, linens, denim, ticking, tough woven cotton and tight weaves are the most practical and useful solutions. Plain colours are the obvious choice, but damasks have a subtle patterning and dramatic animal prints impart a lively mood. The natural, neutral

Above **Natural colours and fibres have an honesty that suits a simple interior. Here, a cushion is fastened with wooden buttons. A pile of fabrics includes hessian, mohair and wool, with bleached cottons and unbleached linens; off-whites, creams, greys and beiges allow a layering of textures and tones. Forest green felted wool cleverly disguises a chair.**

colours of linen and cottons add softness and texture without detracting from the space and are ideal for plain curtain panels and blinds. Cushions add a finishing touch to living areas and bedrooms and provide an opportunity to use pattern. One large or extravagant cushion in suede, faux fur or knitted cashmere retains a simple look without compromising on comfort.

Try to eliminate smaller items, such as occasional tables, that constitute 'clutter'. Wooden chests and carved boxes are popular substitutes and can double up as storage, although a place can always be found for a well-designed generously sized coffee table.

Large tables are not only a place for dining, entertaining and conversation, but also provide a surface on which to work or for children to play at and draw. Tables with a relaxed rather than a formal look offer more possibilities. A contrast of styles achieves a pleasing balance of modern and old – for example, Arne Jacobsen chairs can be combined with an old French country table (see page 88). New designs are straight-edged with a smooth finish, in a range of materials, from dark or very pale wood to metal or glass. Traditional wooden chairs with decorative detailing look casual and characterful and simple modern designs add a little sophistication.

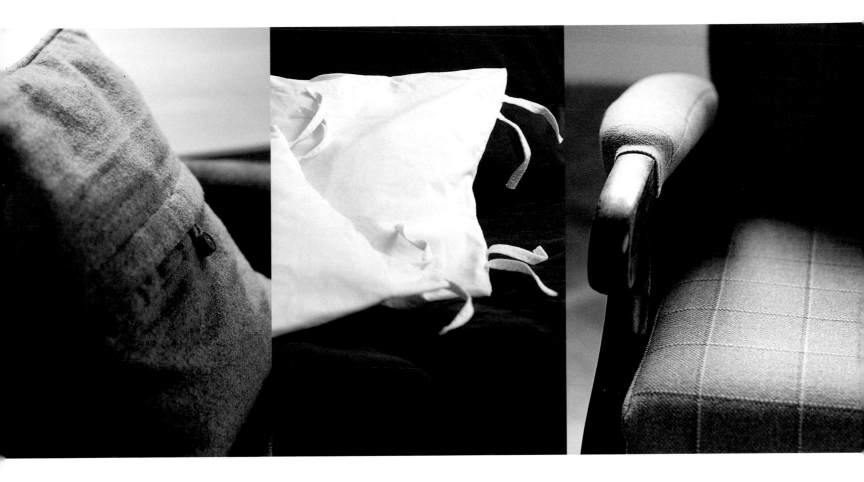

Cupboards with large storage capacities are multifunctional assets, whether they are free-standing or built-in. They can conceal utility equipment, linens and clothes or even an office space. Glass-fronted versions can display objects such as china or glass on the shelves above, while hiding work, toys or less attractive items in the cupboards below. Their presence can be discreet and subtle or imposing and decorative. Despite its size, a huge cupboard in polished wood can look simple when placed in a large airy space with few other distractions.

Innovative solutions to combine sleeping and storage areas include bed recesses built into a wall of units and cupboards built into bedheads or bases. Custom-made bedheads can incorporate wiring for lights and recesses to hold books and personal items. Low-level beds on simple wooden bases work well in areas with low ceilings. Iron beds add a decorative feminine feel to a room and, when stripped back to the bare metal, have a contemporary look. Placing a bed in the centre of the room with storage either incorporated into the unit or provided elsewhere, avoids the need for traditional bedroom furniture, such as wardrobes and dressing tables. However, functional clothes storage in nostalgic or retro styles looks right in a simple setting.

Above **Fabrics add tactile texture to an interior. Piped edges and a single button give interest to a neat cushion. White cotton contrasts with a dark sofa and the cushion cover can be easily removed and laundered to keep it looking fresh. Warm yellow colours of tweed on tailored upholstery blend beautifully with the mellow wood of the chair frame.**

Left **The elegant curves of these 1950s Scandinavian chairs are echoed in a set of hand-carved ethnic stools and a rough-hewn wooden bowl. Warm golden wood tones stand out splendidly and, along with the wood panelling background, help to temper the rigid lines of the stainless-steel table with its white lacquered top.**

Right **On closer inspection, the centre of this whimsical chandelier is a perfectly plain, ordinary spotlight. The unexpected addition of extravagant chandeliers to simple interiors proves that disciplined austerity and pared-down modernism need not be sterile, but benefits from a little romanticism or humour.**

Worn furniture combines an appreciation of the past with a liking for well-used and much-loved items. In addition, the materials and colourings of older or antique pieces have a mellowness and subtlety. Characterful pieces have a strong presence and add substance and personality to an otherwise featureless space.

Contemporary 20th-century design classics have once again found favour. Many mid-century pieces were created at a time when interior design and architecture were very pared down in contrast to the more decorative styles of the previous era. More prosaic products of this era, including sideboards and storage units, have simple shapes and good-quality materials and workmanship. Newly designed modern furniture looks crisp and fresh. The clean edges and smooth surfaces of shiny metal, glass, wood, plastics and lacquered finishes contributes an aura of plain simplicity or sophisticated luxury.

Rich colours, rough textures and organic or irregular shapes of furniture and furnishings add contrast and exuberance, which can lift an otherwise disciplined interior. A single piece of colourful, coarsely woven fabric smooths the sharp edges of a modern sofa and sensuous curves of a hand-carved chair stand out beautifully against a stark background. The pleasure of favourite and beautiful objects is enhanced in simpler surroundings. Unexpected couplings – of antique and new, romantic and hard-edged, pristine and well-worn – work well together and create a unique look and style.

A more relaxed approach to interiors allows for a diverse collection of elements. However, this does not mean that the look is unconsidered. Select pieces for their individual aesthetic qualities and not the fact that they conform to a certain style or scheme. Some furnishings may complement the architectural style of a home, but being historically correct is not essential. Elegant modern furnishings can fit in well with old properties – a contemporary sofa would not look out of place in a rustic barn and, in fact, emphasizes the structure and character of rough walls and wooden beams. Equally, a romantic style of sofa looks stunning set against an exposed brick wall in a converted warehouse.

Above **Beige-grey linen curtains with eyelets slide onto a length of galvanized piping, demonstrating a streamlined window treatment. Plain fabrics and fixtures ensure that the need for comfort and privacy does not detract from a harmonious setting.**

storage

Above **The tall doors and panelled wood of this wall of cupboards means that its function is not immediately obvious. In fact, it conceals essential but less aesthetically pleasing items – a washing machine, refrigerator, cleaning equipment and household files.**

Good storage is as much about organization as about having space. Keeping all evidence of everyday life behind closed doors or cleverly concealed panels is not always necessary and often impossible. Just as some items are best kept hidden, others need to be left on view, either because they are used frequently and need to be accessible or because they are beautiful or well loved and deserve to be on show. Impressive rows of kitchen equipment, shelves of books and treasured objects provide clues to the owner's interests and personality and can be displayed in a variety of ways. Meanwhile, the more mundane and less visually pleasing necessities of life can remain out of sight.

A varied and imaginative approach helps to maximize the area available for storage. When planning a space, consider the options for built-in storage. Allocating one large well-planned and efficient space to storage is generally more preferable to a random collection of smaller cupboards, shelves and containers. A whole wall devoted to cupboards may make a room smaller, but the absence of clutter will make it look and feel bigger. In a kitchen, a wall of cupboards can house everything from the washing machine and dishwasher to utensils and food. Built-in bedroom cupboards keep clothes and accessories orderly and dust-free, and can also store linens, keepsakes and even paperwork.

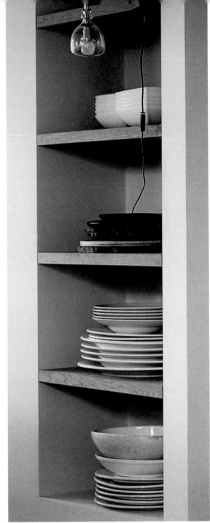

Far left **Here, bright, white space may look serene and disciplined, but full-height doors to the right of the landing, off the stairs, conceal a capacious built-in storage area with spring-loaded cupboard doors.**

Left **Thick slabs of oak fixed into an alcove with concealed fittings make good use of space. A low-key display of everyday china is conveniently placed to serve the adjacent dining area.**

Efficient home offices, work areas and entertainment centres may be successfully incorporated into a wall of storage so that they are completely shut away when not in use. A separate floating wall – either floor-to-ceiling height or lower – can contain storage recesses as well as divide and define different areas of a large open-plan scheme. Doors in the same colour as the wall will meld into the background, becoming virtually invisible. Alternatively, a wall can become a feature if a contrasting colour or finish, such as a dark wood or veneer, is used. Spring-loaded or magnetic door mechanisms allow storage to be concealed behind a discreetly panelled wall.

Storage can be custom-built in alcoves or recesses. Utilizing unused or awkward spaces for storage, such as hallways and under-stair areas, has the added advantage of smoothing out an otherwise uneven or unbalanced space.

Large free-standing cupboards can take the form of magnificent antiques or plain painted units. Paring down the contents of an interior often frees up space for a large piece of storage. Adding shelves, fittings or hanging rails to a cupboard allows a handsome piece to keep belongings safely out of sight but easily accessible, while retaining its use as a feature. Equally effective in living and working areas, kitchens, bedrooms, bathrooms and hallways,

Left **Metal lockers look perfectly at home in this former artist's studio and they provide an unusual alternative to traditional kitchen cupboards. Their grey-blue metal finish is echoed in the dining chairs. An open stainless-steel unit provides a work surface as well as useful storage for kitchen equipment.**

Right **Two cosy-looking bunk beds built into a wall of storage make efficient use of space in this tiny bedroom. The structure creates a charming feature, which evokes the character of the property – a converted barn.**

free-standing units can also be used as space dividers and even bedheads.

Glass-fronted cupboards and cabinets transform storage into display. They can be used to hold treasured collections, china or glass, and a disparate group of objects arranged behind glass doors is more organized than if the pieces were scattered around a room.

Salvaged medical cupboards and gym lockers, usually made of metal, have a sturdy, functional appearance that makes them a novel but useful form of storage. The tall, slim proportions of lockers are suited to small spaces. Ex-library shelving on wheels can be used as room dividers or storage for magazines, books or

cooking equipment. Catering-style shelf units or metal office systems create a businesslike atmosphere, which is thoroughly in tune with loft living. If space is limited, look for units that have sliding doors, rather than conventional doors, which need extra space to swing open.

Combining storage with seating or bedding maximizes space. Low-level shelves can be built as seating along a wall with cabinets underneath. Old settles have generous amounts of stowage beneath their hinged seats and ship's-style, built-in seating can be custom-made with locker space below. Valuable space under a bed can be utilized for storage, either with built-in drawers or large boxes and baskets on castor wheels.

Above A discreet collection of grey laminate cupboards are built into the wall to the left of the sink to keep all the necessary kitchen clutter out of sight. On the open stainless-steel shelves with slate worktop, right, a collection of metal items form a coordinated display. A basic porcelain sink sits on a shelf, with a convenient space below for a galvanized bin on castor wheels.

Right **Old wicker hampers with leather straps provide ample, well-aired storage for linens and off-season clothes, and are ideal for stowing an ever-growing accumulation of children's belongings. They also add an extra surface on which to stack woven plastic hampers filled with items for daily use.**

Beds can be built into a wall or recess, with integrated drawers, cupboards and shelves fitting seamlessly into the surroundings.

Floating shelves, which show no visible signs of support (see page 208), are eminently suited to simple style. They are deep and chunky, surprisingly strong and look modern and pared down. A wall of floating shelves offers a more streamlined way of creating storage and is a feature in itself. Shelves can be dedicated to frequently used necessities, which all members of the household can access. A uniformed collection of buff- or white-coloured boxes or filing folders helps to organize the contents on the shelves; limiting the choice of storage to one type will help to retain a cohesive appearance.

Baskets are characterful, and a large capacious hamper, with or without a lid, can be used to store almost anything. Old, weathered baskets have particularly warm and mellow colourings, which vary with age, the material and the type of weave. A collection, stacked one on top of the other, emphasizes the different textures and tones. Fitted with castors, baskets can be easily transported from one area of the home to another, making them particularly useful for storing laundry, office files or children's toys. Traditional shopping baskets with handles make versatile containers and these too can be easily moved from one location to another. Old leather suitcases, trunks and hatboxes have a similar appeal and usefulness and the natural quality of their materials mixes beautifully with wicker hampers. Large wooden chests and boxes, especially ethnic or antique versions, are often valued possessions in their own right – their storage capacity is an added bonus and they can double up as seating or coffee tables.

A huge selection of inexpensive plastic containers and crates are available in a variety of colours and can be used in an equally large number of ways. Big fine-mesh baskets or plastic crates offer storage for pots and pans, household linens, toys or office equipment.

Above **Window-sills can be utilized in spaces with little built-in storage. White opaque plastic bags hold bathroom necessities. They look neat and organized and ensure that frequently used items are easily accessible.**

Left **Large shopping baskets, used for storing fabrics and wools, offer a casual form of storage under a work table in a bedroom. The tailor's dummy provides an imaginative way to display a favourite necklace and a pretty embroidered throw.**

Part Two

Simple homes

ordered space

The whole of the ground floor of this **smart, modern** townhouse is suffused with light owing to its **open-plan** layout. The space has been divided with carefully placed walls of varying widths and heights and two tall **pivoting glass doors**. Concrete and metal emphasize the architectural qualities of the space and maintain a serene atmosphere in this ordered and well-disciplined interior. The **white walls**, cool grey floor and **modern furniture** are softened and warmed with wood, **natural linens**, woollen textiles and the comfort of an open fire.

oversize doors

The restrained tonal palette of whites, greys and browns established throughout the interior is repeated within the stark animal skull hanging above the fireplace in the living area. The reflective quality of the white walls and the pale, polished concrete floor ensures that none of the light that floods in through the huge windows is wasted. At the entrance to the room, a large glass door is fixed so that it either stands at a 90-degree angle, allowing unimpeded access from the kitchen or it closes (very slowly and quietly) to create a more intimate sitting area.

   The metal-framed sofa, footstool and lamp may be uncompromisingly modern, but the presence of fleece cushions, woollen throws, a soft rug and an old distressed box – which serves as an occasional table – are proof that this is a real home and a place to relax. The fireplace is an elegant, yet functional recess in the wall, with space to store a pleasingly decorative pile of logs. Extending beyond the chimney breast is a low, wide shelf used for displaying paintings, propped against the wall. A tall, slim cupboard unit in pale wood, perfectly proportioned for the space, glows gently in the light that filters through a panel of white linen on the otherwise unadorned window.

The orderly group of condiments, above, conforms beautifully to the colour specifications of this modern kitchen, as does the grey and beige, speckled, terrazzo worktop and the soft beige of the eminently practical tiles. Extra work-surface lighting is provided by circular wall-mounted ceramic fixtures with naked bulbs. A single shelf serves as convenient storage for plates and bowls.

A wall of cupboards in a rich, dark wood veneer, see left, is an unconventional yet sophisticated solution to storage. The units contrast with the hard-edged practicality of the functional kitchen and reinforce the modern aspect of the interior. All the working parts – sink, cooker, refrigerator and so on – are arranged along one side of the room against a tiled dividing wall.

The wall is open at the top to allow light into the space, while keeping kitchen activities out of sight from the living area beyond. A worktop sits on a stainless-steel framework of open units, which house top-quality pots and pans, a dishwasher and a large porcelain sink with an impressive water-spray attachment. Bridging the gap between the two walls is a simple, sturdy kitchen table. Updated by the use of pale bleached wood, the table blends perfectly with the concrete floor below. Chairs in warm tones and a friendly shape, along with the use of large paper lampshades above the table, bring a relaxed, lived-in feel to this family kitchen. The interior demonstrates that it is the use of space and the way objects and elements are put together that denote a style, not the style of individual items.

simple  shelves

Adjacent to the kitchen, which already includes a table for family meals, is a larger, more social, dining room. Two further sets of table and chairs – one for grown-ups and one for children, who also use the area for play – are contained within the space. All the chairs have been painted white to unify the medley of styles. The generous amount of daylight flooding through the windows is diffused by white linen panels tied onto a metal curtain pole. Natural linen curtains, framing the room to either side, are threaded through extra-large eyelets and can be pulled across to provide a more intimate setting. A collection of personal objects and mementos is displayed in an unusual manner on a plank of driftwood hung between the deep windows. Chunky white shelves along one wall show no visible signs of support; they have been fixed to the wall using concealed battens, which allow them to disappear into the white wall behind. A mixture of books, artefacts and children's toys shows that this space is used and enjoyed regularly by all the family.

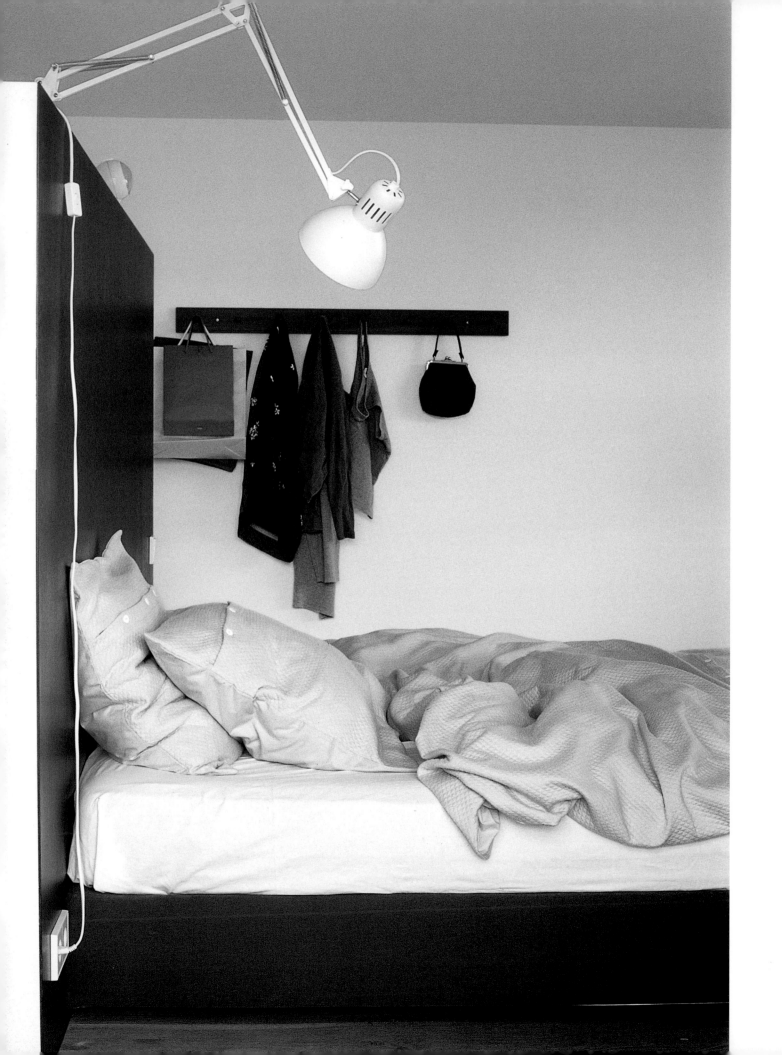

In contrast to the living areas downstairs, the upper floor of the house has a more conventional layout for the bedrooms and bathroom. Space is limited and, although none of the rooms are large, the use of similar elements, including the dark wood veneer, white paintwork and white empty walls, ensures a continuity of style and atmosphere. Instead of concrete – which would be cold and unsuitable for upstairs use (see page 188) – a pale oak wooden floor is used throughout to provide a mellow, relaxing atmosphere, well suited to sleeping.

The master bedroom, shown here, is small, but by placing the bed in the centre, the edges of the room are left free and a sense of space is created. Facing the window is the bed, concealed behind a free-standing wall into which the storage has been incorporated (see page 181). A large cupboard and drawers for clothes storage are all that is visible on entering the room. The furniture and wall, which also doubles as a bedhead, are in the same rich wood veneer as used in the kitchen. Wiring is concealed within the structure and the top edge is used as a shelf to hold bedside reading matter and an adjustable lamp.

The other walls are left free of decoration, except for a row of plain Shaker-style pegs hung with a collection of bags and clothes. An overall impression is maintained of one single structure comprising wall, bed and storage, which literally forms the centrepiece of the room.

The white-only walls and floors in this turn-of-the-century terraced house form a large blank canvas for a delightfully **artistic composition** of furniture, artefacts and treasures. The contents are linked by a strict, but wonderfully muted palette of **earth tones** and accented with the bold and unexpected use of **leopard-print fabric**, animal-skin rugs and large modern paintings. **Organic shapes**, wood in its raw and polished state, stone and old metal form the elements of an intriguing mix of ethnic, industrial, and arts and crafts influences to create an interior that has a touch of **modernity** and a hint of the **bohemian**.

new ethnic

animal prints on white

In a very white interior painting one feature matt black provides an immediate focus. Here, the stark colour of the fireplace also emphasizes the room's elegant proportions and allows for the use of a number of other bold elements. The leather chair echoes the dark colour but, along with the tall floor lamp, provides a very modern look, allowing an integration of two distinct styles within the room. An old chest, painted white to fade into the background, sits in the corner and works well beside the chair and lamp, which are linked by their clean lines and uncomplicated functionality.

White curtains give privacy and warmth without detracting from the contents of the room. The skin rug and animal-print fabric on the daybed are an intriguing mix of ethnic simplicity and contemporary style when seen in juxtaposition with the other distinct features. Their tactile quality introduces softness and comfort to the rather stark interior and their colours echo the palette for the room, bringing the whole cornucopia of styles together. Even the paintings and objects on the mantelpiece conform to the rigours of the dramatically restrained, monochromatic colour scheme.

natural ethnic details

Placing a low cupboard in the centre of the sitting room, where its roughly painted back doubles as a backrest for the daybed, frees up more wall space and maintains the aura of uncluttered calm. The large bookcase could easily have dominated the room, but its white paintwork blends with the walls and turns the books into a decorative display. Similarly, the white frames of a modular collection of small paintings highlight the artworks. An old sack is used as an unusual cushion cover on the leopard-print sofa.

Above, ordinary screws provide support for treasured prints, with their decorative, oriental-inspired frames. The old industrial lamps, found at a local antique store, have retained their weathered patina to give a sense of history to the space. Bark paintings, clipped in place vertically along one kitchen wall, also have a wonderful patina, and their patterns pick up the rich colours of the leopard print used on the sofa. The sculptural simplicity of several handmade wooden bowls, in which fossilized corals are displayed, is enhanced by arranging the bowls individually. Against the simplicity of the colour palette and the pale walls and floors of the space, the details create an artistic feel that emanates throughout the entire home.

No curtains or blinds detract from the splendour of the French windows, far left, which fill the entire end wall of the dining room. As in the rest of the house, the amount of furniture here is kept to a minimum and the white simplicity of the walls and floor allows the contents of the room to stand out. The soft, well-worn outlines of the rustic benches and the intricate curves of a carved stool are highlighted in the glow of light. Two old pub tables have been pushed together

to make one large dining table, which blends perfectly happily with the rush-seated chairs and old, dark wood bench. The industrial scale of the pendant lights complements the proportions of the room, as do the modern paintings, which echo the colours of the wood, stone and metal.

The design of the fireplace is centred around the graceful curves of stone masonry found in an architectural salvage yard. Pieces have been set into the square chimney breast to form an unusual high-level fireplace. A log store supply is recessed below, at floor level. Two more pieces of salvaged stone have been used as brackets to support a zinc shelf in the kitchen, above. The organic nature of this feature provides a rustic contrast to the hard-edged efficiency of the rest of the room, notably the cooker and the inexpensive kitchen units.

new ethnic 69

Limited space in the cloakroom on the left meant that a tiny basin had to be positioned in the hallway. Handy for gardeners and playing children, the basin is small enough to be a discreet presence and doesn't look out of place in its bright white surroundings.

Although the downstairs floor is painted concrete, something softer, quieter and warmer was required for use on the stairs and in the bedrooms. The glowing colour and natural texture of herringbone-weave coir – seen here kept in place on the stairs with slender metal rods – is in harmony with the rest of the house.

Light is allowed into an upstairs bathroom, right, via glazed skylights. Doors have been fitted with etched glass wherever privacy is required. The small space has been cleverly divided using a free-standing wall, behind which are the shower and lavatory. The wall also provides space for two porcelain sinks fixed onto simple metal brackets. Pipework is contained within the structure and the tiled surface incorporates recesses for soap and toothbrushes. A small galvanized metal light, one of a pair, and a wooden stool add a little non-clinical relief.

A 1970s bungalow with a **'50s flavour** invites colourful and comfortable relaxed living. The collection of furniture includes **design classics** in a mix of retro, modern and industrial styles. Here the atmosphere is **deceptively casual**, with much-loved possessions carefully arranged and displayed, but the emphasis is on use and relaxation rather than stylistic rigour. **Texture and pattern** are introduced through a collection of Japanese papers, inventively used as wallcoverings, and furnishing fabrics. The reds, **oranges and warm browns** are typical of the 1950s, as are the straight-edged shapes. Orderly comfort is enhanced by **practical furniture** and fittings for a home that is lived in and loved.

relaxed retro

These curvaceous, moulded plywood dining chairs by Charles and Ray Eames, highly popular in the 1950s, appear here in a wide range of colours and finishes. They have been allowed to retain their character, and their history, giving them an easy, relaxed look that softens the hard, shiny metal of the two modern tables. The tables, which can be pushed together for large gatherings, look less dominant than a single long table and suit the scale of this small dining area, which opens directly from the sitting room.

Although elsewhere there are colourful collections of china, the decision to display only white pieces emphasizes the stark simplicity of the metal medical cabinet, but without detracting from the warm, glowing colours of the chairs.

rows of long shelves

No single style dominates or dictates the look of the kitchen, although the steel cabinets and the cooker possess many of the characteristics associated with functional kitchen design of the 1950s and early 1960s. The stainless steel cupboards are from a medical supplier and fit in unobtrusively among the assortment of styles in this crowded, but disciplined space. A set of chunky wooden shelves provides easy access to frequently used china and glassware and includes a display area for favourite items and collectibles. Practical, easy-to-clean ceramic floor tiles, an old, speckled enamel double sink and a country-style wooden table – which doubles up as a work surface – all contribute to the easy-going mood. The simplicity lies in practicality and lack of fussy detail, rather than in pared-down austerity. The catering-sized cooker and modern, business-like extractor system reveal a pleasure in cooking that overcomes stylish rigour.

versatile sofa units

With its modern shape and construction, the sofa unit is both practical and versatile. The loose covers are made from antique linen sheets and soften the impact of this vast structure, which fills up most of the room. Small animal-hide cushions and a rug add touches of luxury, and lengths of ethnic fabric draped casually over the back of the sofa introduce pattern, texture and colour. Although of different styles and eras, the fabric throws echo the warm tones and patterns of some of the 1950s retro items.

Like much of the furniture in the house, the white-painted bookshelves (with predominantly white contents) were not originally designed for domestic use, but came from a library and can be easily moved around on their large castors. A single pair of candlesticks and a huge mirror stand on a long, low sideboard behind the sofa. With its distressed glass, the mirror adds character, light and an illusion of space to the simply furnished room. The textiles, animal skins and small sculptures are in the same warm tones as the floor, cupboard, mirror and door frames, creating harmony among a mixture of styles.

Sheets of woven fibrous paper pinned to a wall add texture to the bedroom. Less permanent than wallpaper – and much more adventurous – the papers can be easily removed when it is time for a change. Bedlinen, in shades of light lavender with a grey coverlet, and pillows in lavender ticking and grey, harmonize with the dry grassy colour of the wall papers and create layers of subtle tonal texturing on the bed. The elegant retro bedside lamp stands on a 1960s table beside an Art Deco-style clock, proving how well simple classic designs can work together in a space. Although the wire-mesh chair, see right, is a classic 1950s design, the light-filtering, woven-fibre roller blinds and the fibre papers create an overall effect that is Japanese in feel.

woven fibre blinds

colour in geometric designs

The style of furniture in this bedroom, typified by the cupboard and chest of drawers, see left, was, for a time, considered old-fashioned and undesirable, but is now much in demand for its simple, elegant design and the high quality of craftsmanship used in its production. The bedcover has a simple geometric design and the rug contains all the colours used throughout the interior in a paint-box design. Both furnishings are from the same era and make the room look cosy and lived-in. The lamp could be retro or contemporary as the drum-shaped lampshade design is going through a fashion resurgence. However, by placing the two main items of furniture closely together and avoiding fussy extras, the overall effect is simple and contemporary. In the bathroom, the combination of the mosaic-tiled bath and surround, the tiled floor, the matchstick-boarded walls and a large metal jug and wooden bench creates an ambience that is definitely more bathhouse than boudoir. The neutral colours add a subtle warmth, and with the hard edges of a large metal medical cabinet and a simple metal-framed mirror, there is an impression of disciplined ease.

urban country

White is the common factor that **unites the elements** within this country-feel townhouse. Cupboards are used as walls to provide both privacy and storage, and the furniture and fittings add **charm and personality**. While an office is situated on the ground floor, the first floor has been **opened up**, maximizing the light and emphasizing the **feeling of space**, and the kitchen, bathroom and bedrooms are housed on the second floor. This area is dedicated to relaxing, entertaining, socializing and playing. Sociability is the key to the design of the space, with sitting and dining areas divided by a single tall cupboard. Any austerity implied by the white-painted floorboards and unadorned walls is dispelled by an emphasis on communal activity. This is an **easy-going** approach to **family living**.

The dazzling brightness of the interior is tempered by the presence of an over-sized comfortable sofa, two restored and re-covered old chairs and a contented cat. In the uncluttered seating area at one end of this large, open space, exuberant zebra stripes suggest a style that is more relaxed than it may at first appear. The ordinary wooden floorboards have been painted a glossy white to withstand the wear and tear of family life with young children, but they are still reassuringly worn. A pure white table with slender legs sits underneath a large window and supports an elegant, arching table lamp and a delicate glass vase.

There are no curtains and the light is diffused through swing-back fabric shutters of fine, white linen threaded onto metal rods. None of the furniture conforms to a single style and all pieces are covered in various textures of fabric. However, with the pure white background, the overall impression is undeniably simple. The stairs and banisters leading to the kitchen and bedrooms, above, have again been painted white, leaving only the dark metal of the banister rods, which are in a traditional Dutch style.

The whole of the first floor has been opened up to create a spacious living and dining room, well suited to family life. To divide the different functions of the area, a large white cupboard has been used instead of a wall, allowing light to reach into all spaces and creating a more sociable atmosphere. Glassware and white china are stored in the glass-fronted top half of the cupboard, while children's toys are stowed away out of sight in the cupboards underneath.

Rows of chairs – a Danish design classic by Arne Jacobsen – are placed on either side of a simple, country-style wooden table and contrast with the charming selection of small, child-sized chairs. An over-sized bulb light hangs over the table and an old galvanized water butt acts as storage for toys and unwelcome clutter. The old wooden bench serves as the children's table and provides a convenient place for small (and large) people to stand in order to draw on the large blackboard or pin up a favourite picture. In the absence of a fireplace or other distinguishing feature, the blackboard acts as a focus and brings personality and a little humour into the space. White fabric shutters are also used here to maintain the strict discipline of the simple white shell, in which a charming collection of furniture is allowed to stand out.

concrete surfaces

A warm wooden table and old painted café chairs evoke a country feel in the kitchen/dining room on the second floor of the townhouse. Pale, wide, wooden floor planks warm up the cool practicality of the tiled walls and stainless steel oven. The sink and worktops have been cast in concrete and sit on plain, white-painted cupboards (see pages 202–3). Along with the full-height tiled walls and the round metal lights, the concrete creates an efficient catering feel in which any chef would feel at home.

Domestic appliances, including the washing machine, dishwasher, dryer and cleaning equipment, along with all the other unsightly kitchen paraphernalia, are stored behind panelled doors in a whole wall of cupboards behind the table (not shown). The adjustable pendant light above the table is functional and modern, and sharpens up the rustic edges of the table and chairs. Below each window, and above the radiators, a shelf has been built, which can also be used as seating. Space-saving, double-hinged, wooden shutters have been custom-built to fit the windows and maintain the clean lines of the interior.

The country look extends to the bathroom, where an old, battered marble sink, with its characterful re-conditioned antique taps, is built into rustic, cottage-style wooden cupboards in a mixture of reclaimed and new wood. A collection of old-fashioned hinges and knobs adorns the cupboards, which, along with the wood, have been painted white to keep a clean, simple look. The exception is the rectangular mirror frame, which has been painted a warm, pale grey to complement the colours of the marble sink.

A free-standing enamel bath has been stripped down to bare metal on the outside and stands on matt grey painted tiles against a wall of white glazed tiles. The shower curtain is hung from a ring of bare metal above the bath and the new, modern tap and shower attachment ensures an efficient water supply. Since the window overlooks the street, it has been fitted with opaque glass to provide privacy.

marble and wood

white wooden panelling

Wooden panelling adds character to the bedroom, and the walls, floor and paintwork are all white. A bed base has been covered in a textured woven fabric to create a valance and conceal the old divan. The feet of the bed are shiny metal, in contrast to the soft, worn patina of the painted floor. Two small bedside tables have been decorated with silver paint to coordinate with the small metal lamps. The soft mushroom shade of the bedlinen, the only colour in the room, gives a relaxed and restful air. A glass panelled door leads to a walk-in wardrobe, so there is no need for any extra furniture in this fairly small space. The swing-back fabric shutters (see page 195) used throughout the house are also evident here; they provide privacy on this upper floor, but can be opened to make the most of the view.

The rich dark tones of polished wood add a touch of luxury and sophistication to the **disciplined elegance** of this classically proportioned interior. Understated and definitely grown-up, the large townhouse has **high ceilings and tall windows**, giving a wonderful sense of **space and light**, which are teamed with flawless, solid parquet on the ground floor. The straight lines and bold shapes of modern furniture are tempered with **soft textures** in dark charcoal fabrics, the bluey black sheen of pony skin and the curves of hand-carved **ethnic furniture**. Cool efficiency is combined with understated elegance for comfort in a minimalist, yet sumptuous setting for **gracious living**.

modern classic

simple comfort

The classical details of the wall mouldings and the elegant fireplace lend an air of opulence to the sitting room, which is heightened by the use of lush, tactile fabrics, such as the pony skin on the large footstool and the introduction of an intriguing, decorative candelabra. Opulence can be simple if, as here, the walls are unobtrusive and the furnishings are grouped together and kept to plain, but elegant shapes, with materials restricted to those of similar colour intensity. The large, modern sofas are covered in a charcoal woollen fabric, which is also used for the cushions to maintain an understated look. There are no artworks on the walls, but the discreet gold frame of

the mirror above the fireplace, appropriate to the classical features of the surroundings, adorns the room while maintaining the dramatic simplicity. Objects on the mantelpiece have been carefully chosen to fall within the selected colour palette and complement the bold shapes of the furniture. The floor lamp, to one side of the fireplace, is extremely simple and functional, providing necessary light during the evening hours without detracting from the overall look of the room. Rather than making a stylistic statement, the lamp's slender black stand supports a white shade that blends so well with the wall behind that it almost disappears into the background.

modern classic 99

Adjacent to the dining area are two large daybeds with ecru linen loose covers and cosy fleece cushions. They sit on either side of a wonderfully eccentric carved stool and a simple modern floor lamp. The window with doors opening onto the garden has a set of soft linen Roman blinds, which can be adjusted to suit the lighting conditions and will cover the doors when not in use.

To open up the whole space and make the most of the high ceilings with their classical moulded details, the wall beyond the relaxation area has been removed and replaced with a row of slender, square section pillars. Behind these pillars, to the side of the sitting area, a work space has been sited. Contemporary and efficient, it consists of a single worktop along the wall with discreet white storage beneath.

Above the desk, a narrow aluminium shelf carries a collection of favourite photographs and pictures. A state-of-the-art office chair, given a little extra comfort with a furry cushion, and a sleek desk lamp are modern elements. Pale walls and parquet floor unite these two areas for relaxing and working, allowing soft, faintly romantic blinds to work well alongside fitted loose covers, sheepskin and restrained aluminium fittings.

tall columns create work space

Sleek and minimal units, incorporating hob, oven and sink, run along one wall of the kitchen space. No handles spoil the smooth lines of the painted doors and drawers. The surfaces and the sink are constructed of polished concrete. Recessed lighting is discreetly concealed behind a slender, high-level panel to give light to the worktop area below. Opposite, the same basic design forms an island unit, containing further storage and work space. The floor is also polished concrete and extends to the well-appointed dining area in front of a huge window. Only the single child's bentwood chair disobeys the 'right-angles only' rule of the dark solid wood dining table and chairs. A subtle, and slightly whimsical, wall-mounted sculpture in twisted wire offers a little lively relief.

modern classic 103

roman blinds and dark wood

The rich dark tones of the house are followed through into the bedroom and bathroom. A traditional cast-iron radiator sits neatly in a recess below the window, with the water pipes fully hidden inside the wall cavities to maintain a clean look. Thick flannel wool roman blinds in deep charcoal can effectively black out the room, but by keeping the other walls white and unadorned, and by using crisp white bedlinen, the impression is still one of light and space. The dark stain of the waxed floorboards is echoed in the dark wooden unit behind the bed, which, when set against the soft grey wall, creates an atmosphere that is warm and intimate. Simple white-shaded lamps, silhouetted beautifully against the dark wall, stand on a specially-made narrow unit that extends along the full length of the wall. A recessed shelf at the back hides unsightly wires and plugs. The bed, which is on a dark wood platform, is pushed flush against the headboard unit. A stainless-steel door handle, on which a shirt is hung, echoes the light stands behind the bed and is in a modern style that complements the pared-down feel of the room.

An ethnic hand-carved chair in dark wood adds a few elegant curves to the perfect lines of the other furniture within the bathroom. Since all the materials in the space are natural, and therefore compatible, the chair harmonizes well in this setting. It sits in front of another old-fashioned radiator, which is again recessed under a window. A long industrial radiator dries towels hanging from the rail above (see page 97). Mirrors on three sides reflect extra light into the interior, with its dark wooden floor and dramatic marble bath surround.

A bench has been built alongside the bath to provide a useful area for drying, dressing and storing towels at bathtime. The bathroom doubles as a dressing room; wall panels behind the bench and bath conceal cupboards which are used for storing clothes. The honey-coloured veneer of the wood allows the spring-loaded cupboard doors to blend with the warm-coloured marble of the basin and also prevents the space from becoming too dark. A pair of basins has been formed by cutting a wedge from a single, slender slab of marble. Minimalist taps, fixed above, with the pipework hidden behind the wall, enhance the simplicity of the design. A wooden venetian blind provides essential privacy, while filtering the light into this luxurious room.

invisible bathroom storage

The simplicity of this **rustic retreat** lies in the use of raw materials and textures. Its affinity with the **surrounding landscape** is confirmed by the limitless versions of the subtle hues of nature. The greys, blues and greens of earth, sky and foliage are reflected in **hand-dyed textiles** and weathered paint. Bare walls, unfinished wood, natural fabrics and the **honest simplicity** of plain country furniture form the basis of a highly individual style, centred around nature and imbued with a **touch of nostalgia**. A fascinating harmony of the relaxed and the casual, combined with creativity and a delight in the essence of simple country living, is enhanced by an ever-changing supply of **natural decorative objects**.

raw texture

The simplest of storage solutions, from pigeonholes to wonderfully battered old cupboards, house all the kitchenware in this homely kitchen. Samples of dyed linen fabric, in shades of loam and lichen, hang from metal clips on lengths of wire running along the top of the undecorated plaster walls. More fabric is fixed behind a basic wire dish drainer. Elsewhere the walls are mottled with traces of old paint, in contrast to the pristine white door frames.

In the dining area, the mellow, well-worn wood of the sturdy tables and chairs stands out against the white walls and the old painted floorboards. A console table holds a collection of everyday plates and old-fashioned steel cutlery. Beneath, a stout galvanized box is used to store files and papers. The wooden fire surround made from salvaged wood rests against the wall where a fireplace was once housed. A pretty romantic chandelier, with its cascade of glass droplets, disguises an ordinary functional bulb. A similar unadorned bulb forms the shape of an elemental table lamp. Two wall-mounted candle sconces complete a trio of contrasting light sources that nevertheless work happily together. A length of white muslin, pinned across the window, filters out harsh sunshine when necessary.

natural artworks

and modern lights

Another salvaged fireplace, see left, rests against the wall to provide a focal point and give the illusion of a real fireplace in the centrally-heated sitting room. In front of the fireplace, wood kindling is placed in an open-weave metal basket as a purely decorative feature. Walls have been painted an aqua-grey and then splattered with a thicker white gesso to give a textured finish. The paint effect complements the bare wood of the ceiling and the roughness of a low painted table, which has been created from a rustic old door.

Traditional gingham checks of the loosely fitting home-made covers look bold and fresh and link the sofa and chairs, although they are of different styles and scales. The walls are relatively uncluttered, but a display of pressed seaweeds, mounted onto individual sheets of paper, has been pinned to a framed board and propped on the small table that serves as a desk. A quirky task light, with long wires that emerge from a metal bar, accompanies an idiosyncratic mix of personal objects.

Coarse-weave fabrics, hessian, homespun checks and fine antique linens have been hand dyed in natural vegetable colours to create a highly textured sampling of cushion covers. A semifitted beige linen cover on the sofa covers the seat cushions, too, keeping the comfortable, squashy shape in order. The large, plump cushions on top of the sofa are made from linens and ticking that have been dyed to create an old rustic look, and are stuffed with wool fleece.

A screen behind the sofa consists of old patinated planks of wood joined and hinged to make an unconventional backing board on which pictures and natural objects have been hung. The boards look wonderfully weathered and worn, with several shades of greeny greys revealed through different layers of paint. A single, modern spotlight is fixed to one of the planks, with its cable and plug hidden out of sight round the back. An ordinary round table has been painted to fit in perfectly with the surroundings.

Many of the pieces have been purchased from flea markets or local shops, and finished with an artistic eye to highlight their inherent qualities. The interior achieves a simple style by celebrating the natural rawness of materials and the signs of use and wear, which reveal myriad tones, shades and textures in every surface.

The bedrooms are calmer, gentler and more feminine than the other rooms in the home. Blue is the predominant colour in the child's bedroom, left, where the white painted bed stands out beautifully against plain, pale blue walls. The bedlinens are a mixture of homespun plains, tickings and checks in a range of hues, from the softest baby blue of the pillows to the deeper blue of the gingham-checked coverlet. On top of an old painted chest is a charming doll's house, which is also painted a complementary blue. The floor is a more mellow colour, with residues of blue paint giving it an antique look. In the master bedroom, above, an old metal bedstead is covered in a citrus-yellow, hand-dyed linen and is piled with silk damask and ticking pillows. The wall is painted in the same soft grey as the damask cushion cover and has been decorated with a pattern of delicate white stencilling. A metal ring attached to the ceiling supports a narrow length of delicately embroidered voile, which drapes over both ends of the bed.

natural white

Restrained femininity and **traditional style** combine to create a serene, grown-up atmosphere. Lavish and uncompromising use of white paint achieves an illusion of **endless space** in this small Long Island cottage and draws attention to the elegantly detailed panelling on walls, doors and fireplaces. The walls are kept bare and the **beautifully proportioned**, traditional sash windows are left uncovered or have **simple white** shutters. The white-on-white of painted furniture, bone china and loose covers is combined with a highly **disciplined palette** of the natural rich browns found in **honey-coloured leather**, well-polished wood and a collection of wicker baskets that have been darkened by age.

The bare beams, stripped wooden floor and coir rug impart a wonderful warmth to this sunny room. Glossy white shutters on the windows can be adjusted, section by section, to control the light and provide privacy. When closed at night, they meld into the walls and become virtually invisible. Glossy white paint, used on all the woodwork, reflects the light, making this small room feel spacious, clean and bright. The large, comfortable sofa and armchair are covered in white washable cotton, giving a freshly laundered look. A leather armchair varies the texture and adds warmth.

The panelling of the elegant fireplace extends across the wall, losing none of its distinctiveness by being painted white, and kindling for the open fire is kept in a white pot at the edge of the hearth. Two candle holders, four tiny white bowls and a white-framed round mirror on the mantelpiece are the only ornamentation in the room, except for a tall white lamp. A simple folding bench is used as a coffee table, but can be folded away to increase space. Next to the sofa, a recess in the wall is fitted with floor-to-ceiling bookshelves.

bone china and painted wood

Apart from the bleached pine floorboards, absolutely everything in the dining area is white, including the china on display, the lighting fixtures and the table decorations. The inexpensive chairs and the plain table have been gloss painted; a basic enamelled metal shade hangs above. Light floods in through the sash window, which has been left bare to add to the purity of the space. The use of brilliant white-on-white creates a pristine, scrubbed look, seen on everything from the walls and windows to the shelves and the candlesticks. Cream-coloured Wedgwood bone china, see above, stands out against the slightly cooler tone of the wall. The chunky design of the shelf and brackets is in sympathy with the rest of the wood detailing.

The kitchen space is small but, with its unadorned windows, full of light. A dining area is separated from the kitchen by a narrow, slender metal table with a slate top. This forms a visual division between the two areas, as well as a physical barrier, and provides storage for a small selection of baskets. Terracotta herb pots conform to the stringency of the colour code and their scale makes them a feature rather than a decoration. A tall cupboard, painted white, is also in keeping with the style of the house and enables less-disciplined clutter to stay safely out of sight. The bowls on top of the cupboard make the room look less austere and much more lived-in. The white sink, worktop and storage units are practical, unfussy and unprecious. No attempt has been made to disguise the dishwasher or the 1950s-style cooker; instead, the impression is of efficiency and practicality. Above the work surfaces, a single open shelf on graceful brackets holds clear glass and ivory china. A beautiful collection of variously patterned white plates are displayed in an antique rack, far right.

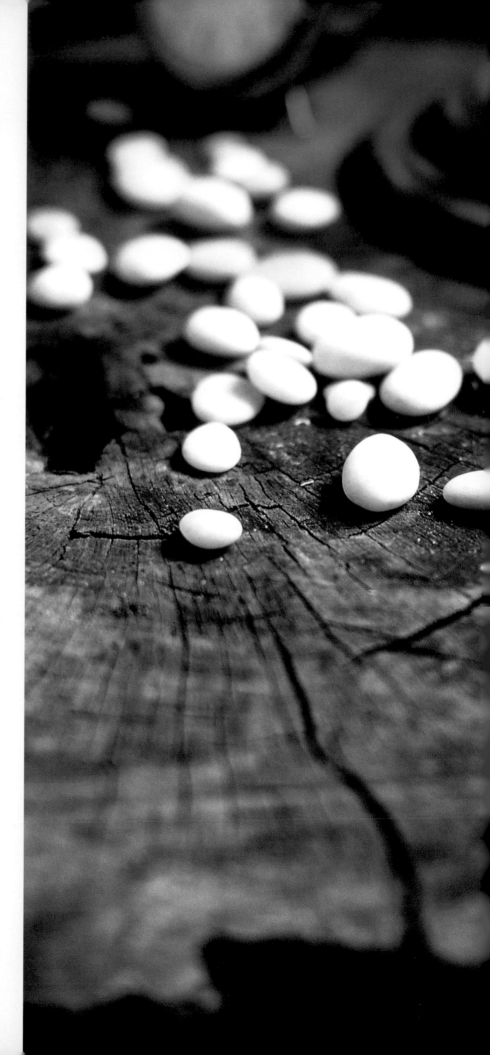

Windows on two sides of a tiny bedroom allow an abundance of light to enter. Once again, simple white shutters have been used, which will become part of the unadorned walls when closed. The four-section design of the shutters – with their subtle panel detailing – offers the opportunity to adjust the light levels and create different moods.

A large section of tree trunk, which takes the use of natural materials in this interior to an extreme, makes an intriguing bedside table. This rough, quirky piece contrasts with, and softens, the immaculate look of the room and adds character. Smooth white pebbles, collected from a nearby beach, emphasize the rough texture and interesting patterns of the sawn timber.

The graceful antique sleigh bed takes up most of the space in the bedroom. The smooth, polished wood of the bed adheres to the strict colour discipline of the house. An abundance of pillows and the fine, white, antique bedlinens completes the picture of calm comfort. A charming, old-fashioned lamp base adds a feminine touch and connects with the polished wood of the bed. As in the rest of the house, a serene atmosphere is maintained with minimal amounts of furniture and the limited palette of white and natural wood.

walk-in storage

A tall country-style chest of drawers, left, has been painted the palest of greys, allowing it to stand out against the whites of the wall, shutters and door in the bedroom. On top is an antique plate filled with jewellery and treasures. The room remains completely clutter-free, thanks to a walk-in dressing room leading off the space. Highly organized with shelves and rails, the dressing room provides storage for clothing, shoes and accessories. As expected, the bathroom is white, but here the accent colour is a gentle natural linen, which complements the pale wood and basketweave. The glass-fronted cupboard contains a suitably restrained collection of bathroom requisites; those less visually pleasing are stored in baskets. A length of natural linen has been fixed around the basin with Velcro for easy laundering. The linen hides the pipework, which would otherwise spoil the clean lines established by the rest of the contents, and creates a useful hidden storage space. A double row of white pegs offers easy accessibility to towels.

This **traditional home** is brought to life with a bold but composed use of colour. Walls and furnishings are painted in **chalky shades** of peppermint, sky blue, blushing pink, bright red and yellow. Although a wide **range of colours** has been used throughout, each of the rooms is based around one main colour, with walls and furnishings in similar or complementary shades. The grandeur of high ceilings and tall windows is further enhanced by **romantic furnishings**, gilded mirrors and chandeliers, but these are combined with **simple country** furniture, much of it restored and given a new life with colour. Bare **wooden floors** and a carefully edited selection of furniture, pictures and possessions allow the coloured walls to create ambience without dominating the space.

composed colour

All the radiators, exposed pipework and even the light switches have been painted the same colour as the walls in the house so that they blend into the background. This creates a less cluttered look and allows a focus to be created only when it is required. A small chequerboard painting in sky blue and white coordinates beautifully here. The pale wood of the Swedish bench complements the stripped floor, while the soft pinks of the cushions are echoed in the bold flower painting hanging above. A large dining table (see page 130) is covered with a generous purple gingham-check tablecloth, with the corners tied to the table legs for neatness. The tall windows are uncovered for maximum light and dramatic effect. With its adventurous use of colour, the room nevertheless retains a restful ambience, owing to the similar pastel tones in the pinks of the fabrics and the blues of the paintwork – all the colours are echoed in the paintings. By using pale wood for the floor and furniture, the effect is simple yet stunning.

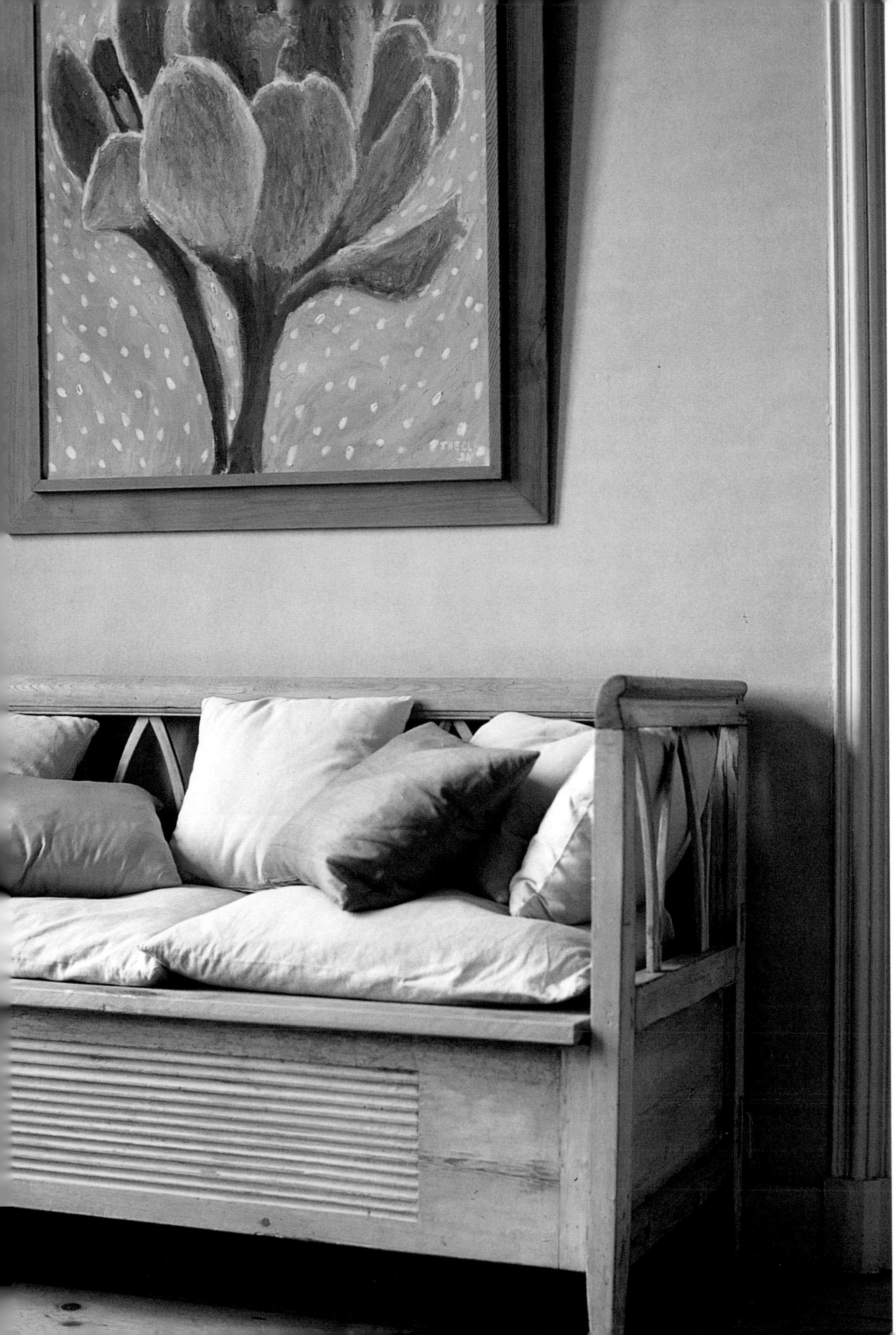

pastel shades and wood

The glowing pink walls of the sitting room enhance the grandeur of the black marble fire surround and gilded mirror hanging above. A rather grand, gilded French chair is covered in a delicate cream damask, outlined with bold upholstery tacks. On the mantelpiece, a delightfully eccentric collection of Chinese pots and bouquets of metal foliage add a decorative touch. A black piano harmonizes with the marble of the fireplace and connects with the colour of the picture frames, above. The Swedish country chair looks homely and witty with its brilliant floral-covered seat.

In another, smaller, dining room, see right, the window frames and shutters are painted in bright glossy red and the walls (not shown) are a strong yellow. The chairs are a lighter red and the table is luminous tangerine. This riot of colour is controlled by a strict adherence to the red/yellow zone of the spectrum and the unity of texture provided by using gloss paint. The decorative nature of the table and wrought-iron chandelier are countered by simple café chairs on a bare floor.

bedroom and study

Two decorative sleigh beds have been painted in a pale sky blue that is only a shade darker than the walls, so that they almost become part of the shell of the room. Their pretty feminine shape stands out as a feature through the use of bright green gingham covers and vivid pink floral pillowcases, which are in character with the rest of the house. Clip-on lamps are modern and practical, and also demonstrate how successfully the romantic can be mixed with the functional to give a contemporary feel. The stripped wooden surface of an old desk echoes the bare, unpolished wood of the floorboards. The desk's shape has the right combination of straight lines and curves to fit in well with the beds, but its unsophisticated, rustic nature is also appropriate to the pared-down simplicity of the room. A child's oil painting, propped casually against the wall, introduces pattern and links with the mix of homespun checks and country floral bedlinens.

On the ground floor of this **former farmhouse**, the walls dividing the kitchen, dining and sitting areas stop short of the edges to allow an all-round **light to penetrate** the space and turn cooking, eating and relaxing into companionable activities. In order to maximize the space in this way, the library adjacent to the kitchen is closed off with imposing **glazed metal** doors. Colour is confined to the **natural hues** of oak, concrete, polished wood, sisal matting, marble and distressed zinc. The kitchen, library and small cloakroom all have concrete tiled floors laid in a **chequerboard pattern**, formed by alternate tiles being turned at right angles. Upstairs the area is cleverly divided to create the **illusion of space**, despite sloping ceilings and restricted headroom. The open layout, subdued palette and minimal use of furniture give a sculptural feel.

open house

A shelf has been built around two sides of this kitchen to provide storage, display and seating. Keeping the outside walls free of fixtures and fittings gives the space an airy feel. All the workings of the kitchen are integrated into a large island unit with a dark grey, shiny marble worktop. Wiring and pipework is concealed beneath the concrete floor, and the large extractor fan above also incorporates an efficient modern lighting system. The walls and paintwork are pure white, and the splendid windows have been left bare, except for rectangles of fine white fabric pinned to the lower half. Incorporated into the dividing wall between the kitchen and dining areas is an open-fire grill, accessible from both sides. On either side of the grill and recessed into the deep wall, solid, oiled oak shelves offer convenient storage.

marble-topped island unit

The full effect of the unusual layout, which uses shortened partition walls (see page 181), can be seen here. In more conventional interiors with full-width walls, the light would have been restricted to just one of these two windows. All-day light floods in around the edges of the walls, creating a special atmosphere.

Colours in the room are restricted to natural tones. A large daybed is covered in chocolate-coloured brushed cotton. Its clean lines and tailored cover complement the straight, sharp edges of the inexpensive occasional table, which has been paint-washed and then finished with a thick layer of varnish and combed to give a textural, ethnic effect. Both pieces of furniture sit on a large sisal rug, edged in grey cotton, which adds warmth and texture to the surroundings.

The floor lamp is a slim metal rod topped with a tiny shade. Though all the outside walls are white, the wall directly behind the daybed has been painted a subtle beige. Since there are no pictures or artefacts, the addition of a little colour breaks up the space and makes it more intimate. Beige also emphasizes the architectural structure of the space. The television is on castor wheels and can be moved easily between the different areas.

Another, more traditional, sofa is unashamedly comfortable. Its grey-brown upholstery looks wonderful against the creamy beige-washed wall. The sculptural, stepped design on one side of the staircase, see right, allows in more light, preventing the stairs from being boxed in, and provides visual variety. Pale oak stairs link with the oak flooring in other areas of the house. The wrought-iron handrail, supported on small, discreet brackets, is slender and elegant with shepherd's crook finials.

The dining room, see above, has immediate access to the kitchen, so there is no need for any furniture other than the table and chairs. The dark hardwood, country-style dining table comes from India, but the rough-and-ready surface has been polished to make it smooth and bring out the rich tones of the wood. Michael Thonet bentwood chairs have darkened with age and look loved and cared for. The pale oak floor has been sealed with a matt finish and the skirting board adds a modern-looking touch to the edges of the floor.

This tiny room in the eaves makes maximum use of all the space, despite sloping ceilings. Beams have been left exposed for a little extra height as well as visual interest. The bed is on a specially-made low base to allow for headroom. In order to incorporate a good-sized bathroom into the space and allow natural light into both areas, a low plaster partition has been built, which has a console table on the bed side and a bath on the other. The bath is built into a distressed zinc 'box' built onto the low wall, which also contains the concealed pipework for the minimal taps. There is a step up to the bath area, which creates additional storage for pipework. Two porcelain sinks stand on a cantilevered,

distressed-zinc plinth, each with its own mirror and light. Taps emerge directly from the wall and the mirrors have been set into the plaster for a sleek look. Both are positioned on the only full-height wall, which provides privacy for the shower behind. Pendant lights have clear glass shades to reflect light; they are suitably functional for a bathroom but add a touch of elegance. Throughout the space the floor is luxurious, honey-coloured stone. The bathroom area receives natural daylight and ventilation from the windows, but the use of the low partition wall means that the sleeping area, sited towards the back of the space, still benefits from the window light.

authentic country

The white-washed walls, exposed beams and bare floors associated with traditional **country dwellings** are all present in this farmhouse. A mix of old and new furniture, **workaday fabrics**, natural floors, light walls and highlights of colour enhance the character of this family home. Downstairs, the white walls, oak floors and original **stone flags** form a perfect background for blue denim upholstery, bleached linen curtains, large old cupboards and brightly coloured, modern dining chairs. Upstairs, coir matting and bleached or **painted floorboards** give a warmer feel, with the occasional coloured wall and use of boldly striped and checked fabrics. Seasonal variations are subtly catered for, with the addition of double curtains and the comfort of an **open fire** in winter, and a profusion of **sunlight** in summer.

Although all the ingredients of a traditional farmhouse kitchen are present, this room maintains an air of serenity. Warm oak floor is sealed for practicality and the built-in butler's sink is flanked by wooden draining boards. The country-style cupboards and the free-standing work bench are painted white, with highlights of colour provided by small elements within the room. A contemporary feel is achieved through the use of a white (but eminently practical) vinyl table cover and a set of modern chairs. Ivory walls, beams and door and window frames keep the overall look clean and simple.

Glassware, china, utensils and food are stored out of sight. Evidence of cooking and preparing food can be seen in the collection of chopping boards behind the sink, a display of kitchen knives on the wall and stacks of professional-style pots and pans stored on the shelf below the work bench. This is a family kitchen, the hub of the house, and a favourite place for entertaining visitors. The sleek, lacquered plywood chairs in pink and red, based on a classic Scandinavian design, are comfortable for everyday use, yet sophisticated enough for dinner parties. Metal shades hanging above the table are from the local farm supply store. They are inexpensive and can be seen in dairies and outbuildings on farms throughout the countryside. Instead of paintings or photographs, a large blackboard provides an ever-changing range of impromptu artwork.

With its associations with work- and leisure-wear, denim is the perfect fabric for life in the country. It makes an unusual but practical upholstery material, which is also complemented by the rugged textures of the old flagstones. Casual-fit loose covers on the chairs and sofa have been washed several times and, like well-loved jeans, look and feel better with age. The infinite variety of shades from the deep indigo of new to the pale whiteness of the well-worn, give denim its special character, which is here nicely emphasized by the different shapes of the two old chairs. A Chesterfield sofa, opposite, looks comfortable and relaxed in its fitted denim cover. The blue cover is easily washable and has developed a charming faded softness over time. A frilled valance adds a flirtatious look and a

brightens a light space

humorous touch. Squashy cushions with envelope and tied covers continue the blue theme in denim and patterned weaves. As a contrast, another working fabric, blue-and-white striped ticking, has been used for the footstool. The neutral tones of the coir rug blend with the flagstones and its chunky texture is well suited to the character of the home, as is the functional and inexpensive work lamp. Curtains made from linen sheets are stitched to old-fashioned rings and hang from a plain metal rod. In winter, a strip of Velcro stitched to the back of the linen enables a panel of canvas to be attached, providing discreet additional insulation. Keeping the walls, curtains and table white and using only blue on the upholstery leaves the room light and gives focus to an old dark wooden cupboard.

painted wood and nature displays

The surrounding countryside affords a rich supply of found objects. A 'nature table' is an old farmhouse table painted in off-white eggshell – a warmer white adds spaciousness without introducing coldness in low-ceilinged farmhouses such as this. Apart from a large white jug, the table is kept clear of small clutter in order to maximize the impact of a dramatically large seed head. The dry browns and greys of the plant harmonize with the rich, dark wood of the cupboard and the soft grey of the original flagstones.

A large fireplace is set in an inglenook with flagstone-topped benches to each side. The shapely mantel and the bricks forming the sides have been painted white to blend in with the walls; the colour also emphasizes the sooty blackness of the fireplace. A monochrome collection of black-and-white photographs stands on the mantlepiece. A side table is painted white, giving its traditional shape a contemporary feel. Here the table holds piles of books and a single white jug of freshly-picked poppy heads.

A traditional metal bed, found in a local antique shop, has been stripped of its old layers of paint to reveal its surprisingly slender construction. It stands on the bare floor as the centrepiece to the master bedroom. Any austerity suggested by the stark bedstead is softened by the gentle colour and warm texture of the bleached floorboards. The red and white of the bold striped ticking curtains is echoed in the stylized floral-print pillowcases and the flower-patterned quilt that acts as a valance. A large, tactile faux fur throw offers extra comfort for chillier nights. An old, white linen cloth covers a rather ordinary bedside table. To maintain an uncluttered environment, the pictures and a wooden-framed mirror lean against the walls, rather than being wall-hung, and a convenient walk-in wardrobe keeps clothes and accessories out of sight. Modern bedside lamps on plain metal stems blend comfortably with the surroundings, as does the elegant table lamp on the white work table that also serves as a baby-changing area.

grey metal and papered walls

The bathroom makes the most of its country-style atmosphere, small size and situation away from the rest of the house with a bold use of wallpaper. Its exuberant pattern is a modern design based on seaweed and sea urchin shapes in shades of lilac and grey, enhanced with silver. The rest of the room is, however, strictly limited to shades of white and metal. Tongue-and-groove boarding, painted white, helps to maintain a balance between pattern and plain. An old-fashioned bath and basin have reconditioned taps from the same era and the basin stands on a newly built, plain panelled cupboard. A glass-fronted cupboard and small washstand were bought locally. Their pretty decorative details are kept in check with the use of white paint and by limiting the material of all accessories to functional metal, which is echoed in the metal lampshade hanging overhead. The washstand is topped with a slab of marble to complement the greys of the wallpaper, the patina of an old galvanized container and a collection of pebbles and shells.

White floor paint provides a hard-wearing surface for the two young occupants of this bedroom. An old laundry basket, fixed with industrial castors, serves as a large mobile toy box. A red wall and red gingham fabric, in different-sized checks for bedding and curtains, add a cheerful, lively spirit to the room. Red is repeated in the child-sized rush-seated chairs, with the rest of the furniture in the room painted white. The tall cupboard holds all the children's clothes and a wicker hamper keeps other items well out of reach. A small table provides a place for a night light and a propped-up noticeboard, which is also covered in red gingham.

Curtains hung on metal rings from a plain metal rod are quilted for cosiness and generous in length to keep out draughts. The canopy of the four-poster bed is in khaki denim, which is edged and tied to the frame with red string, giving it a tent-like look. Its side panel has two large pockets sewn on the inside to provide a handy storage place for books, teddies and other treasures. A 1950s cot in a traditional style is pleasingly simple with its original paint finish. The children have a separate playroom in the house, where all their essential toys, games and art materials are stored; in contrast, the bedroom is for sleeping and its quiet simplicity provides a suitably calm atmosphere.

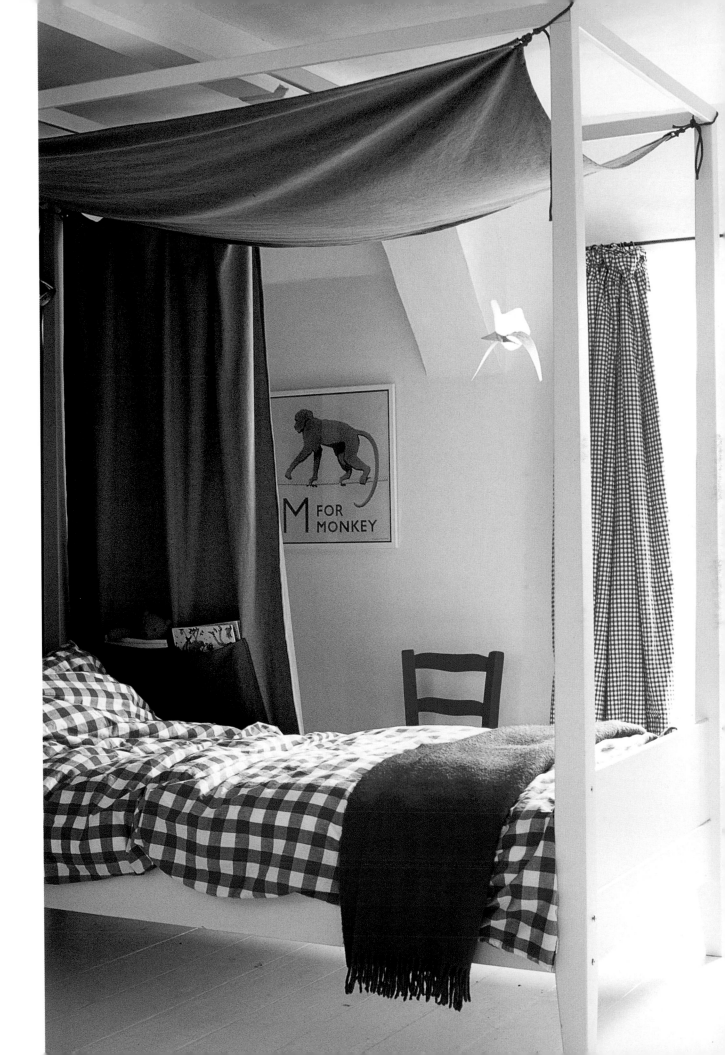

mellowed antique

The warm earth colours and antique furniture create a comfortable, well-established and **timeless ambience** in this elegant country house. Bleached wood and terracotta-tiled floors blend with creamy beige walls and the pinky tinge of partly-stripped doors. The **pared-down furniture** mixes traditional country pieces with soft upholstered fabric in shades of muted raspberry reds and florals. Dusky tones of the **terracotta floor** in the library harmonize with the **faded covers** of old books on the floor-to-ceiling bookshelves. Aged tints and bold geometrics of a display of antique chessboards reflect the **rustic nature** and disciplined qualities of this interior.

The fireplace provides focus in the library. A floral-print chair stands out beautifully against the bare, tiled floor; its bright colour adds a contrast to the more muted tones. One wall and the old beamed ceiling (seen reflected in the antique mirror above the mantelpiece) have been painted white to lighten the space and lead on to the sitting room, shown right. The creamy beige walls of the sitting room complement the warm red of the sofa and give a restful, luxurious mood. A piece of antique floral fabric draped across the sofa reinforces the colour theme and adds femininity. No attempt has been made to repair the damage to the simple fire surround, shown above: function is more important than style in this home. A large, gilded mirror is romantic and reflects more light into the space. No curtains interfere with the elegant proportions of the tall French windows, which open out onto the garden; instead, outdoor shutters are used to provide privacy at night. The 1960s floor light is an unexpected addition to this antique-filled interior, but helps to maintain a contemporary feel.

Elegantly proportioned double doors lead from the sitting room to a small study, seen left. Doors have been partially stripped to leave a wonderful patina of layers of paint and wood, which match the terracotta tiles. The slim framework of the metal trestles corresponds with the slender glazing bars of the tall window in this light-filled work space. On the desk, piles of magazines have been arranged to exhibit their wittily appropriate chequerboard spines. The kitchen walls, above, are washed with several layers of pinky terracotta to build up a rich surface in earthy depths of colour. This wall colour and finish, along with the large kitchen table and stool, would have been a familiar sight in simple rustic dwellings of the past. A stout oak shelf holds a selection of white china and the inexpensive clip-on lamp illuminates the black terrazzo sink and work surface. The pale, bleached-wood finish of the floor and the plain-fronted cupboards and drawers emphasizes the natural grain and character of the material. A large catering-size cooker looks efficient and practical, and its proportions work perfectly in the space. The ceiling has been painted off-white to reflect light flooding in from a large window.

Space is the main component of this house, which has been formed as a **pale shell** that allows the carefully-edited mix of old and modern either to stand out from or to dissolve into the background. **Disciplined and restrained** use of mainly white furnishings has enabled the romanticism of crystal chandeliers and traditional furniture to be successfully combined with the pared-down, stark simplicity of modern style and the **organic shapes** of ethnic and Scandinavian looks. The generous and elegant proportions of the rooms, doors and windows are enhanced by the **uncluttered environment** and the use of stark white and a pale aqua. Subtle tones and textures are provided by **natural fabrics** and controlled accents of more saturated hues appear as cushions and floor coverings.

pure and elemental

fireplace and candles

The lower-ground floor, housing the dining, kitchen and living areas, presents an overall look of white, metal and wood. A log fire burns on a base of loose bricks laid on top of concrete. Without a grate, and with its old rough bricks, the fireplace is minimal and natural, and offers an area of texture to otherwise plain walls. Together with a decorative display of logs and a wire basket of kindling, the fireplace warms this uncompromisingly minimal space that serves as the dining room. Concealed lighting, set behind narrow panels at the top of the alcoves on either side of the fire, throws a wash of subtle light down the walls. The sleek, organic curves of the dining chairs – a classic Danish design from 1950 – provide a contrast of shape and colour, and soften the hard edges of the table and bare white walls. A brushed-steel table, with a white-painted wooden top, links with the lampshades hanging above. The large, spun-aluminium lampshades reflect the white and the light, and their scale marks them as a feature rather than an accessory. A collection of nightlights, set into tiny hand-moulded porcelain dishes, are arranged on the table. They can be used for candlelight meals in front of the fire, turning this pristine white room into a dramatic space of flickering, warm colour.

The furniture in this room is kept long and low to emphasize the high ceilings. Plain linen curtains have been attached to clip-rings and hung from white-painted metal poles, which are discreetly fixed onto the ceiling moulding. Two modern daybeds, one with integrated tables that extend on both sides, contrast with the soft, relaxed shape of the sofa. One daybed has a loosely covered, feather mattress to pad the shape and add extra comfort when it doubles as a guest bed. Two pouffes, one in thick white linen and the other in creamy beige suede, conform to the low profile of the furniture. The floor and woodwork have been painted white, but the walls are a pale, watery, washed aqua. An open fireplace offers warmth without intruding into the clean lines of the space. Sky blue, silk cushion covers are decorated with a cyanotype print of leaf silhouettes.

The comfort of natural fibres, in the form of textured bedlinen and a warm, pale grey felt rug, contribute to a restful atmosphere in the bedroom. A hint of beige on the walls lessens the starkness of the bare walls and painted floorboards. The shutters are made from Perspex, hinged onto the architraving, which diffuse the light through its milky white translucency. Similarly, the paper bedside lamp gives a soft, intimate light. Two bentwood stools – another classic Scandinavian design – act as

bedside tables. Opposite the end of the bed is another open fireplace (not shown). The bedroom opens into an adjacent dressing room, seen overleaf, where clothes are folded onto open Perspex shelves and hung from Perspex hooks. A tall, narrow wooden unit houses towels and linens – all in regulation white. Another set of narrow wooden shutters, this time floor-length and painted, provide visual interest as well as complete privacy, and can be folded back to allow light to enter the room.

Part Three

Making it happen

getting started

The essence of simple style is paring down, avoiding unnecessary clutter and creating an easy-to-live in, comfortable home environment. It isn't necessarily about minimalism, so don't feel you have to keep everything out of sight. Deciding on a specific look for your home will depend on personal taste, the existing property, your lifestyle and the cost. An interior that reflects your own personality and passions is preferable to the sterility of a slavish dedication to a style.

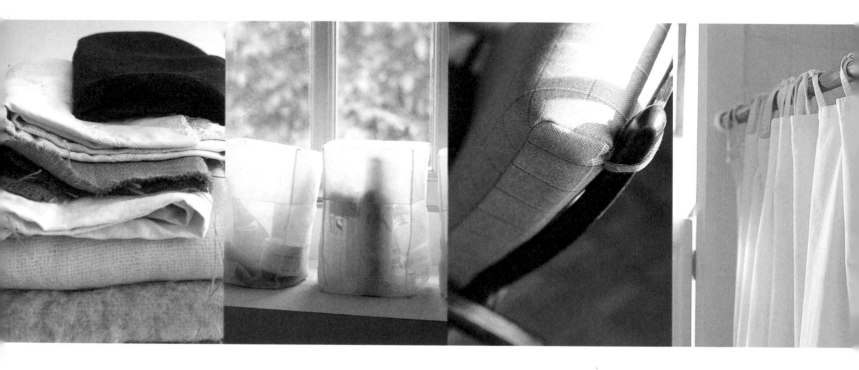

The selection of products and materials for domestic interiors has increased in the last few years. Most towns have shops and showrooms that offer a comprehensive range of kitchen and bathroom fittings, flooring, heating and lighting, as well as furniture and accessories. Antique shops and markets have also widened their scope to include newly-fashionable retro items and many 20th-century design classics. Floors, walls, windows, fitted furniture and fixtures form the shell of the interior, providing the essential backdrop for simple style. Using a restrained and consistent palette, an interior can be unified to create a feeling of space and harmony. Furnishings, essential equipment and accessories, as well as your personal possessions, will enhance the space and add character. For ideas, look at books and magazines and visit showrooms, museums and art galleries, but also take note of public and commercial buildings. Inspiration can come from unexpected sources – for instance, a colour scheme can be based on a favourite painting or a collection of pebbles.

Stripping back

To provide the 'blank canvas', or shell, on which to plan your interior, get back to the basic structural elements of floors, walls and ceilings. Stripping out old or unattractive furnishings and fittings will fully reveal the shape and structure of the space, highlighting previously unseen or unnoticed good features, as well as more negative aspects. Decide what can be disguised or ignored and what really needs changing. If you are fortunate enough to have large spaces, well-proportioned rooms, beautiful windows and attractive architectural detailing, then these features can be emphasized. If, on the other hand, your home is less distinguished, then keep the interior plain and make a statement with furniture and accessories.

Some properties may have been 'improved' by the addition of poor-quality fixtures or the removal of original features, and this can be remedied. However, don't feel you have to be historically correct – taking away original mouldings and detailing can enhance the inherent architecture. Also, don't be tempted to introduce 'character' with old-style skirting boards, architraves and doors. Rather than imposing a particular style on the space, let the space dictate your decisions.

Floors should be unified, but can consist of different materials. If possible, take up all old floor coverings. The condition of the floor beneath will reveal any unsuitable surfaces. You may find original floor tiles, flagstones, parquet or good-quality floorboards deemed unfashionable by the previous occupants. Such a lucky discovery could form the basis of the style, colours and materials used elsewhere. If the floor is rough concrete or chipped tiles, consider floating a self-levelling screed over it to give a smooth, level surface, ready for applying a new covering, such as stone, vinyl or rubber tiles.

Walls can be easily redecorated, but a good surface is necessary. Strip away old wallpaper and wall coverings, and take off any unwanted tiles. If old tiles are in very good condition and unusual, they are worthy of repair and restoration.

Getting back to the bare plaster will ensure that such problems as cracks, damp patches and rough finishes can be corrected. Wash and scrub the walls to remove traces of old paste, which may react with paint and cause discolouration. Lining paper covers flaws and gives a smooth base for paint, but imperfections are often characterful, particularly in older properties.

Paintwork on doors, window frames, architraves and skirting boards can usually be washed down with a proprietary product and repainted. If the build-up of old paint masks the curves of mouldings, you may need to use a paint stripper to reveal the detailing. Old paint may be lead-based, so it is best to leave it stable rather than sanding it down. Bare wood will need priming before painting and several new water-based, quick-drying products are available. Old and damaged paintwork can also be primed to produce a smooth, stable surface.

Fixtures can be replaced, but think carefully before taking out any piece that was included in the original interior; often these form part of the

all-white shell

contrasting textures

character of the building and are correctly proportioned.

Strip out any badly made or superfluous kitchen units, cupboards and shelves. Consider replacing or removing unattractive doors, or using quality panelled versions in a period home. Boxed-in pipework sometimes spoils the clean lines of a room, so unless it forms part of the structure or the workmanship is of very high quality, remove it. Revealing the pipes may look better and create a more spacious feel, especially if they are painted the same colour as the walls. If exposed pipes detract from the space, re-route them or conceal them within new structures.

Windows can be costly and impractical to change. Consider replacing frames if the old ones are in poor condition or not in the original style or material. Make sure that new windows are the correct style and proportion for your property – inappropriate window

frames can have a detrimental effect on the price of your home. As windows are part of the structure of the building, consult an architect or builder before carrying out any work.

Editing possessions

Unless you are starting from scratch or have a large budget, you will already have furnishings and belongings that need to be incorporated into the available space. The simple style approach involves creating a pared-down environment, so be prepared to edit down your possessions.

Discard or give away anything you don't need or like, or that doesn't work, is beyond repair or uncomfortable. Dispose of any inefficient or unwieldy storage units. Keep items you love, that are beautiful or full of character, and hold onto anything that is useful. Try to look at familiar items in a new way. Cleaning, repairing, repainting or reupholstering can give new life to a piece.

floor plans

assessing the
space

professional
advice

Planning

Space, or the illusion of space, is an important aspect of simple style. The size and style of your home may impose certain limitations, but consider new ways of dividing up and using the space you already have. Knocking down interior walls or using floating walls may seem attractive options, but think carefully before committing to an open-plan scheme – family life sometimes benefits from having small private areas for different activities. Consider what is going to work for you, as well as styles that inspire you. Don't get carried away with a visual idea without considering the practicalities first. Moving into the home before redesigning will allow you to discover how sun positions, access paths and your day-to-day needs influence the space, and may help you to avoid expensive mistakes. Using a scale plan of a room or the whole area will enable you to see how the space can be reorganized and how the furniture fits into the plan. An architect will produce a detailed, technical plan, but you can make a simple drawing to help you see how your arrangements and ideas will work.

shower

full-height floating walls

sinks

console table

bed

low floating wall

bath

Left and above **In order to have a larger living space downstairs, a bedroom with an integral bathroom has been fitted into the opened-up roof void. The floor of the bathroom area is raised to conceal the pipework beneath. A limestone tiled floor is used throughout.**

Floor plans

Measure a room carefully and draw it up on squared paper – the bigger the scale, the better. Draw in doors and their opening areas and mark the positions of windows, radiators, sockets, fitted cupboards, fixtures and light fittings. Fit each room into a floor plan to build up a master plan.

Make templates of your main furniture, measuring at their widest points and using the same scale as the room drawing. Arrange them on your plan. Furniture often takes up a lot of space and you will need to allow for outstretched legs on sofas and armchairs and enough room for pulling out, as well as sitting on, chairs around a table. Also bear in mind the space needed for opening cupboard doors and drawers.

Assessing the space

Look at how best you can use and divide up the space and experiment with ideas on your plan. Opening up the whole of one floor to create a large area for cooking, eating and relaxing can work well. Simply removing doors can give a more open feel and easier access to living areas, though you will need to adhere to fire regulations. Consider unconventional ideas, such as 'floating' walls, using a cupboard as a dividing wall or placing furniture in the centre of a room.

New stud partition walls can be easily constructed from a timber or metal framework, covered with plasterboard, plywood or wood panelling, and then finished with plaster, paint or veneer. For stability, a floating wall will need to be fixed at some point to the floor or ceiling.

It isn't always necessary to carry out extensive building works to substantially change how you use

space. Look at the way rooms are allocated and used. Traditionally, the kitchen and living spaces are downstairs and the bedrooms above, but upstairs rooms are often lighter and sunnier with better views, so consider reversing the layout. Don't feel you have to finalize every detail – allow for a lucky find or a bright idea.

Professional advice

If you are considering structural alterations involving demolishing walls or enlarging openings, it is important to consult an expert first and get planning permission if necessary. Taking away structural walls requires a supporting beam to prevent the building, or parts of it, from falling down. An architect, structural engineer or building surveyor will do the necessary calculations. When planning changes, it is worth employing an architect as they offer professional advice as well as innovative ideas. Architects' fees normally include supervision of the building work and they may recommend qualified and skilled builders.

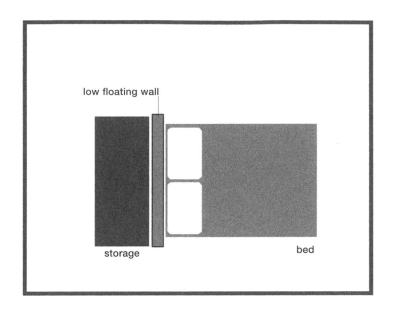

low floating wall

storage

bed

Left and below **By placing the bed and clothes storage in the centre of the room, on either side of a floating wall, this average-sized bedroom looks much more spacious.**

Materials

Collect swatches, samples and pictures of all the materials you are considering using, so that you can see how the colours and textures work together. Most shops and manufacturers will supply samples on request. Make a collage using the materials, as well as examples of your existing possessions. If you have a computer drawing program, you can quickly produce simple plans and scan in swatches and pictures of furniture. This can also be a good way to try out different colours and see how they change the mood and scale of a room.

Limiting the number of elements, materials and colours will keep the interior looking simple and increase the feeling of spaciousness. Naturally finished woods and stone blend harmoniously, and when used with shades of white or neutrals will provide a tranquil backdrop. Dark surfaces, such as slate, marble or wood, add accent and sophistication, but use them carefully and consistently. Flashes of colour will brighten an environment, but for best results, use no more than two colours in a room. Make the most of different shades and tones of hues.

Surfaces

Materials for floors, worktops, walls, fixtures and fittings are available in a comprehensive selection, including many products previously used commercially. Keep in mind how one room opens onto another, and choose surfaces that make a sympathetic transition.

Floor surfaces are available in a huge selection of wood and wood finishes, as well as stone and the increasingly popular concrete. Alternatively, there are vinyls, linoleum, rubber and various carpetings, including coir and seagrass, as well as wool.

Worktops in marble and slate, zinc, stainless steel and concrete are frequently used in addition to the ever-expanding range of solid woods and laminates.

Fixtures and fittings for kitchen units, sinks, appliances, bathroom fittings, taps and lighting are widely available in a choice of different materials, colours, styles and finishes. Even inexpensive ranges now offer stainless steel, coloured enamels and surfaces once considered purely at the luxury end of the market.

Furniture

Consider how your existing pieces will work with newer additions. Old and antique furniture often has attractive polished wood, stripped metal or patinated surfaces. Matt-finished pale or dark woods, shiny- and satin-finish metal, plastics and glass are prevalent in more modern furnishings. Leather looks warm and mellow when old, and soft and sensuous when new.

Fabrics

Natural linens and cottons, soft wools, flannels and felted wools are all ideal for a simple style approach. Faux furs and velvet add a tactile comfort. Using similar tones for all soft furnishings will maintain an understated look, but the addition of dramatic animal prints or colours can inject spirit and personality into a room.

Paints

Several paint ranges feature beautifully subtle shades and traditional-style finishes. Many of these paints tend to be denser and more matt than commercial paints. Their characteristics are reflected in the colours, which tend to be more muted and similar in tone. As these edited ranges all share similar qualities, they naturally work well together. When used throughout an interior, they will create a unifying feel, even if the colours are quite different. Larger commercial companies are now producing similar ranges, presented in various themes or moods to make choosing colours much easier.

tonal paint colours

Neutral palette

Neutrals are the colours of nature and harmonize well when used for surfaces and soft furnishings. They offer an infinite variety of tones and textures, from the dark intensity of granite grey to the mellow softness of creamy off-white and from coarse-weave linen fabrics to smooth felted wools.

White and denim blue

As timeless and comfortable as a much-loved and well-worn pair of jeans teamed with a crisp white shirt, denim and white will fit in with any style of interior. Denim fades and softens with use, so keep it in focus by combining it with fresh white paint. Blue-and-white stripes also add a touch of contrast.

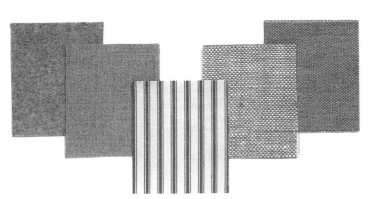

Red and white

Flashes of red add accent and definition to a predominantly white or neutral interior. Solid red should be used sparingly, but simple stripes and gingham checks, especially when used for curtains or bedlinen, look cheerful and warm.

Floors

The desire for a more open, airy and spacious feel in interiors has led to the resurgence of 'bare' floors. The most frequently used material is wood, and a wide choice, from professionally laid, solid wood block to inexpensive laminates, is available. The natural properties of wood add character and warmth to a space. Limestone has become increasingly popular, as more varieties are now available and methods of laying less complex. Concrete, traditionally a base for other forms of flooring, has become a valued material in its own right and is perfect for a modern look. Although these forms of flooring can be expensive, they are a permanent feature that, when properly installed, will add to the quality and value of your home. As bare floors are part of the structure, rather than an added component, they contribute to the pared-down elemental ethos of the simple look.

Your choice will depend on budget, the existing floor, suitability of the structure and the position of your home. Take care to choose a reputable company – getting it wrong can be potentially disastrous, both structurally and financially. Remember too that bare floors are noisy. If you live in an upstairs flat or loft, your lease may stipulate that carpet must be laid for maximum sound insulation. Covered floors in a colour or material that complements the interior can give a similar bare look and may be used successfully alongside wood, stone or concrete.

parquet
laminates
floorboards
wood finishes

Parquet

Traditional solid or parquet floors are constructed from thick blocks of wood, such as oak, birch, cherry, mahogany or teak, often arranged in a herringbone pattern. New solid-block floors are expensive, but will last for many years and will improve with age. Usually they are laid onto concrete, with a damp-proof membrane inserted between the layers, and they should be professionally installed. Less expensive, thinner varieties can be laid on top of existing floors. They are a viable alternative, providing they are installed correctly, though some have an unnatural, easy-care finish.

Old block floors can look dark and dull and may have loose or missing blocks, but repairing them is a worthwhile option. Sanding, oiling and waxing can also help to restore them to their former glory.

Laminates

Laminated floors are popular as they are inexpensive and relatively easy to lay. Sold in lengths or sections, the newer versions do not require gluing, but lock together and can be laid onto your existing floorboards. Ready-finished and usually stain-resistant, they are hard-wearing and easy to maintain.

Their composition varies; some feature real wood veneer, while others have a synthetic wood finish or metal effect. Some synthetics are unpleasant to the touch and unconvincing to the eye. It can be difficult to distinguish between real wood veneer and acrylic, but the composition should be stated on in-store labelling or on packaging.

Despite the accessibility and apparent ease of use, research before you buy. Laminate can swell and lift if subjected to contact with water; avoid using it in kitchens and bathrooms unless specified as suitable for these areas. The non-porous finish of some laminates can cause a build-up of condensation in the floor cavity below, with the consequent development of dry rot. Make sure there is adequate ventilation and consult an expert or the manufacturer if necessary.

Applying a liquid product for laminates, consisting of wax with various additives, will help maintain a seal and minimize wear.

Floorboards

Wooden floorboards are the most common type of flooring, and existing boards in good condition are relatively easy to clean and treat. A variety of woods and widths are available, from inexpensive narrow pine boards, originally intended to be covered, to wide hardwood planks with attractive grains.

New floors can be laid using new or reclaimed wood. New wood has an even colour, texture and size, and is easy to work on. Usually, these are tongue-and-groove, and as they have no gaps between the boards, they make efficient and easy-to-clean flooring. Reclaimed wood is less consistent in size and quality, but has the advantage of an aged patina and inherent character. Reclaimed boards may require a considerable amount of preparation, both before and after laying, and extra is needed, as wastage can be up to 30 per cent.

On original floorboards or reclaimed wood, sanding will remove dirt, old varnish and paint, restore the character and reveal the grain of the wood. Large gaps can be filled with strips of wood or filler.

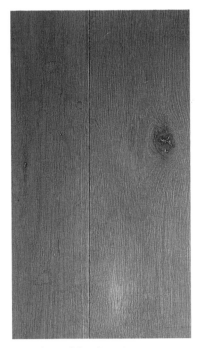

natural wood floorboards

parquet

pale oak floorboards

painted white floorboards

Although replacing a damaged floorboard is fairly simple, if the overall condition is poor, a new floor should be installed, preferably by a professional. The techniques can be complex and mistakes are difficult and costly to rectify. If you decide to lay the floor yourself, do plenty of research first and discuss the job with your local builders' merchant or timber yard.

Wood finishes

All wood needs treating to protect the surface and prevent it from becoming dirty and discoloured. Depending on the look you require, the location and the type of floor, finishes include oiling, waxing, bleaching, staining and painting, as well as varnishes for sealing.

Most of the following treatments and finishes can be done yourself, but take time to research all of the available techniques and finishes first before deciding which to use. Some may be inappropriate for your existing materials and space, and can be difficult to remove if you do not like the result.

For all the processes, make sure you follow the health and safety recommendations for the materials you use. Wear protective gloves and a mask when using varnishes and paints, and ensure the whole house is well ventilated, as well as the room being worked on. Always read the manufacturer's information on the container before buying to ensure that you get the correct product to suit the condition and composition of your particular floor.

Sanding wooden floors removes old varnish, wax, dirt and minor imperfections, leaving a smooth, clean surface ready for treatment. Industrial sanders are available for hire, but it is always a dusty and messy business, so make careful preparations. Check there are no protruding nails or debris which may damage the sander. Ensure the room is well ventilated and wear a mask to avoid breathing in the dust. Hanging a dampened dust sheet over the outside of the door will prevent some of the dust escaping to other areas.

Varnishes and sealants are necessary for a hard-wearing surface, suitable for heavy use. A wide range of polyurethane varnishes and sealants are available in different colours and stains, and in matt or shiny finishes. These products can be used directly on new wood, or on freshly sanded or cleaned wood. They can also seal stained or painted floors.

Efficiency and quick-drying properties are constantly being improved. However, speed isn't always everything, and sometimes the natural look is sacrificed in favour of ease of application. Even clear varnish will have an effect on the floor colour, so test the varnish first in an inconspicuous area.

Waxing and oiling new wood prevents the wood from drying out and allows the floor to cope with day-to-day wear. Oil is the traditional treatment for wood flooring, with wax applied for further protection and to produce a mellow surface sheen.

Apply oil on new porous wood, so that it sinks into the surface. Oils such as teak, linseed and Danish oil will feed the floor, keeping it supple and scuff-free. Wax can be used as a finish itself or to preserve another finish. Apply the oil or wax by brush or cloth, depending on the manufacturer's recommendations, but have cloths available to wipe away any surplus.

For a soft shine, wax can be buffed after application using a lint-free cloth or a soft brush. Professional electric buffers can also be hired for large areas. Wax in liquid form is easiest to apply and several proprietary brands are available. Regularly oil and wax wood surfaces, especially on areas of heavy traffic and wear, to build up a self-protecting seal.

Staining floors brings out the grain and gives character to the wood, but will also highlight blemishes and imperfections. Wood stains are available in various finishes and colours. Dark stains and colours look dramatic, but they can make a room appear smaller.

Stains should be applied to a clean surface without any traces of old varnish or wax. They soak quickly into the wood and must be applied evenly to avoid a patchy effect. Be sure to do a small test in an inconspicuous area first, as colour will vary depending on the existing wood and, once applied, stains cannot be removed.

Bleaching gives a wonderfully pale, clean look to floorboards and also provides a soft and gentle surface that is kind to bare feet, making it particularly suitable for bedrooms. However, bleaching is not suitable for high-wear areas as it absorbs dirt easily.

The process requires a new or freshly sanded floor and the bleaching technique must be commenced as soon as possible to avoid any orangey tinge to the wood. There are various products available, most of which are based on soap with an added whitening agent, which is washed into the floor to produce the bleached effect. Cleaning is done when necessary using just the soap.

An alternative to bleaching is a limed effect, where the grain of the wood is emphasized by rubbing in a colour, usually white. There are several 'liming' products available,

original stone

slate floor tiles

but you could get a similar effect by painting the floor with diluted emulsion paint and then rubbing down the surface with fine-grade sandpaper to leave only the paint that has soaked into the grain. Seal with a matt varnish to keep it clean.

Painting gives an overall flat finish and will cover imperfections in the wood surface. Specialized floor paint, available in a wide range of colours, has good covering properties and will produce a tough, robust surface that is easy to clean. An attractive worn look will develop in time, or the floor can be repainted if you prefer a new-looking effect. Painted floors can be slippery, especially in bathrooms, so make sure that any rugs or mats are secured with anti-slip devices.

For a soft, paint-washed look, use specialized decorators' paints or emulsion. Water-based paints will soak into the wood and do not contain any plastics, which may

react adversely with the hardeners in varnish. Seal a painted floor with wax or varnish. Clear varnish applied on top of white paint tends to create a yellow tinge, so use floor paint for a pure white finish. Wax applied on top of a painted floor will give a mellow 'aged' look, but will need regular applications to prevent the paint becoming dirty.

Stone

Stone is a beautiful and practical material. Derived from the earth, its inherent qualities and colourings bring a natural harmony to an interior. The soft, matt finish is part of the appeal of stone, but polished stone surfaces also have their own character and provide a practical and sophisticated alternative.

Stone is unaffected by water (and flooding), making it particularly suitable for use in kitchens and bathrooms. It is, however, an unforgiving material – anything dropped onto it will probably break.

Also, as it does not absorb sound, it can be noisy, so think carefully before using it in a large area, especially where there are other hard flooring surfaces.

Old stone floors imbue a sense of history to the homes in which they are found. Original flagstones may be uneven in texture and size and their colour varies according to the stone (usually local) used. New stone flooring is available in a wide variety of colourings, slab sizes, shapes and finishes, from pale limestones to dark granites.

As stone is quarried from the earth, its colour, character and properties will depend on geological factors. To the untrained eye, one piece of stone may look the same as another, but an expert will be able to distinguish good-quality stone from inferior. New stone is supplied in a variety of sizes, from standard tiles to slabs suited to large areas. Always consult, and buy your stone from, a recommended retailer or supplier.

Installing a new stone floor is best done by a professional. The veining and natural colour variations that occur in some materials mean careful blending is required to give a natural-looking finish.

A level screed base is necessary for laying stone, though it can also be laid onto a sprung floor. The traditional method of laying slabs on a bed of sand and cement has mostly been replaced with the use of adhesives. Joints are grouted after laying and for sprung floors, the adhesives and grout have flexible additives to allow for movement. Polished stone will normally be repolished after laying to provide a smooth, even surface.

Maintaining and caring for stone is easy. When stone is first quarried, it is relatively soft, but it starts to oxidize and become harder and less porous when exposed to air.

After laying, a stone surface is treated with a generous application of a silicon-based impregnator, which reduces the porosity. Regular washing with a neutral soap will feed as well as clean the stone. Matt finishes will develop a patina with use, but after approximately two years, oxidizing and constant walking over the surface will have encouraged the formation of a hard surface layer that is resistant to stains. At this point, the stone starts to 'look after itself', needing very little cleaning and maintenance.

Limestone is currently popular for its pale creamy tones, although greys, deeper colours and speckled or randomly-marked surfaces are also available. It is smooth to the touch and polished. One newly developed finish involves burning off the surface and polishing it with nylon brushes to leave raised areas that have smooth edges.

Slate has a natural distinctive 'cleft' texture, which looks rugged and adds character to country-style properties and dramatic contrast to modern interiors. It can also be obtained with a smooth surface. Although available in different colours, including black, green, red, purple and multicolours, the most sympathetic to a simple interior are the traditional greys, which range from charcoal to a whitish pale.

Marble is solidified limestone – it has turned to liquid in the earth before hardening again. It is usually

mosaic

concrete tiles

associated with a distinctive pattern of veining, which can vary from the subtle blends of pale hues to more dramatic slashes of contrasting colours. As well as the familiar whites, greys, greens and blues, there are warmer pinks and beiges.

Terrazzo

Terrazzo is formed of a mixture of marble aggregates, cements and pigments that give it a distinctive, speckly appearance. The enormous variety of finishes and colours is created by varying the size and colour of the marble pieces as well as the amount of pigment.

The original method of applying terrazzo as a single slab, on site, created problems of shrinkage and cracking. Today, a more stable surface is achieved using pre-cast and pre-polished tiles or units. As with stone, the tiles can be fixed with adhesive or by the more traditional method of setting tiles onto a bed of sand and cement.

The terrazzo used in public buildings often has large pieces of aggregate in contrasting colours, but far more subtle finishes, which are more suited to domestic use, are also available.

Ceramic

Ceramic floor tiles are usually made from compressed porcelain fired to very high temperatures, which produces a hard-wearing, waterproof material with a consistent appearance. They are thicker and more robust than ceramic wall tiles. The shiny, glazed finish gives a clean, hard-edged look, especially when used with wall tiles in a similar colour and finish (see page 190). Matt-finish tiles are now being produced in convincing imitations of stone, marble and terrazzo, as well as a range of subtle finishes and plain colours.

Cheaper and less porous than stone, ceramic tiles are more consistent in size and colour.

Although they lack the character derived from the natural imperfections of stone, their evenness produces a smart, pristine look in a room.

For showers or areas where water is present, use a waterproof grout. If the surface beneath is flexible in any way, the grouted joints can pull away, allowing water to penetrate. The floor may need lengths of solid wood inserted between the joists to reduce movement and sheets of plywood fixed on top to ensure a level surface. If the consequences of water seepage are potentially catastrophic, incorporating a damp-proof membrane into the construction is advisable.

painted concrete

polished concrete

Quarry tiles are a traditional form of ceramic tile with a dense, matt finish, usually in terracotta or dark brown, though they are also available in off-white. Old tiles have a pleasantly worn look, whereas new ones provide a flat, even-coloured finish. Quarry tiles are traditionally laid onto a bed of mortar, but adhesives can be used. As with all tiles, a level concrete surface is best, but new adhesives and flexible additives in grout allow tiles to be laid onto other surfaces.

Mosaic

Mosaic tiles are small versions of ceramic tiles and are often used for more decorative work. Pre-formed mosaic, often in unsubtle colourings and inappropriate materials, has lessened in appeal. However, natural stone, ceramic and glass mosaic tiles can be used to give a highly sophisticated and subtle look. Complicated patterns should be avoided, but a simple design

applied around the edge of flooring can be effective. Used in kitchens and bathrooms, stone and matt ceramic mosaics will have a natural appearance, and translucent glass looks elegant in bathrooms.

Concrete

Concrete forms the ideal base for many floor finishes, but can also be used as a material on its own. It is especially appropriate for modern and industrial looks, but used boldly and confidently can look good in any interior, especially if installed throughout one level.

Whiteners are often added to cement, but pigments are also available to produce a variety of finishes, from a solid colour to a more random effect. A polished finish, where the concrete is floated level and then 'polished' by repeated trowelling, looks stunning and is highly practical.

Information on installing and finishing all types of concrete

projects is readily available from professional organizations. It is possible to carry out the work yourself, but seeking professional advice is recommended. The weight of the material makes it suitable for ground floors and basements only, unless the floor is reinforced, as in homes converted from industrial buildings. To support concrete slabs, the floor must be level, well-consolidated and firm, so it won't move and settle, causing the concrete to crack. Several products are available to ensure that the concrete dries out properly and professional advice should be sought, as it is important to use the right product at the right time.

The concrete can be sealed with an acrylic resin as soon as it has hardened, but most treatments are applied after 28 days. Once dry, the surface can be painted. Floor paint (see page 186) will cover well, but new products are constantly being developed.

Floor coverings

Replacing or installing new floors is not always possible for practical or cost reasons, and wood or hard floors may be too cold or noisy to suit your living arrangements. However, a dramatic change in the style of your home can be achieved with floor coverings, which may also add warmth and comfort. Plain coverings, used throughout a space, will link different areas and form a simple, unobtrusive background. Keep the look uncluttered by choosing one material that can be used in most of the rooms, adding softer surfaces, such as carpeting and rugs, where desired. If you decide to use more than one type of covering, choose complementary colours and finishes to maintain an impression of unified space. A number of floor finishes previously considered suitable for only kitchens and bathrooms, such as stone and concrete, are now popular in general living areas. Vinyl and rubber flooring, especially in tile form, can be successfully used for all rooms. The neutral tones and natural texture of sisal, coir and seagrass matting is conducive to a calm ambience and can work in country-style settings, as well as more modern environments. Fitted carpet is quiet, warm and comfortable, as well as cost-effective. Although unsuitable for kitchens or bathrooms, it can blend effectively with other floor finishes.

Linoleum

Linoleum is made from a mixture of natural materials, including wood flour, linseed oil, pigments and natural resins, which give it a distinctive marbling pattern. Used extensively from Victorian times to the mid-20th century, it then went out of fashion as newer materials became available and fitted carpet was more affordable. In more recent years, linoleum has become popular in multicoloured floor designs and it is produced by a large number of specialist manufacturers (see page 214).

Appreciated for its natural ingredients, subtle colouring and matt finish, linoleum looks best as a single colour. Careful laying, using adhesive, on a smooth, sound surface is required, and this is best accomplished by a professional.

Vinyl

Vinyl is often thought of as a less expensive and more hard-wearing form of linoleum, and certain types are now considered unfashionable. It is easy to clean and cool underfoot. Inexpensive varieties are available in sheet form and need no adhesive. The available designs tend to be a little complicated, but plain terrazzo-effect and chequerboard patterns are simple and neutral enough to work well. More expensive and sophisticated vinyl floorings are available in a selection of colours, patterns and finishes, including imitations of terracotta, stone and wood. If a simple design is chosen, vinyl can be used to stunning effect.

Vinyl needs to be laid onto a completely flat and even surface, such as a self-levelling screed or a layer of hardboard, so that the imperfections or texture of the floor beneath do not show or cause wear. Tidy cutting and laying is necessary to avoid badly fitting edges, creases and buckling. Avoid vinyl for large areas, as unsightly joins may be needed. In these cases, choose vinyl tiles, which will need to be secured with adhesive.

Rubber

Rubber is warm, practical and good for sound insulation. Widely used in schools, hospitals and sports clubs, it is robust with a fashionably matt finish. The range of plain colours makes it popular for domestic use; however, it can be expensive. Although a number of treatments are available to seal the surface, rubber will mark easily. Blemishes and indentations may not show up in a large commercial building, but may be more noticeable in a domestic setting.

Natural coverings

This form of floor covering, which includes sisal, coir, seagrass and jute, is the natural alternative to carpeting. All varieties are spun from plant fibre. The appeal of these materials is their distinctive textures. Their natural appearance and neutral colouring makes them ideal for the simple style approach, as they blend with wood and gently contrast with pale walls.

Woven in a variety of patterns, from flat weaves to bolder herringbones, some types feature colourful stripes or borders. In addition to a range of widths for fitting wall-to-wall, there are also rugs and narrow runners for stairs, which can be edged with cotton tape, leather, suede or felt.

Although hard-wearing, the coarse textures can be unfriendly on bare feet, especially for young children. However, finer and tighter weaves are smoother and some coir and seagrass has a softer feel. Versions using wool, linen, cotton and other smoother fibres have more recently become available.

Maintenance can be a problem with these coverings, as dirt is not easily removed and accidental spills can stick between the fibres. Many woven coverings are pre-treated with a stain-resistant finish and newer weaves and treatments make them less prone to dirt. Some sisal rugs are reversible and can be turned over once one side is dirty. Being a natural product, the floor coverings will wear and mature in an attractive way.

Carpet

Bare floors can be cold and noisy, and carpeting provides quiet luxury at a price that is often far below other floor treatments. Carpet can also add a touch of warmth to harder floor surfaces or announce a change of setting in a space.

Wool is traditional, warm, comfortable, durable and easy to maintain. Cords and subtle woven textures in neutral and soft natural colours, including beige and grey, are the best choices for a simple look. Dark colours make rooms appear smaller and will also show dust and fluff, but can introduce a change of mood or a touch of drama in spacious homes.

Carpet neatens the look of a staircase and cuts down on noise at the same time. For a light look, or a bit of contrast, use a narrow runner with plain metal stair rods. Alternatively, buy carpet pads, which are fixed only to the steps – this option is ideal for beautiful wooden or painted staircases.

Walls

Plain, pale walls and paintwork will enhance the feeling of space and provide a smooth backdrop for more textured furnishings. Using the same colour or tones throughout keeps the look simple and unifies a collection of small rooms. Although white or off-white walls are the favoured choice, they are not compulsory. Subtle tints, bold hues and careful use of wallpaper, paint effects and stencilling can provide an accent, focus or inject a change of mood in an interior. Bare walls create a serene, uncluttered impression and allow other features, such as architectural detailing, materials and furnishings, to stand out. Light also reflects better off plain walls.

A good surface is necessary for the application and finished appearance of paint. With large areas of plain wall, any imperfections will show, so repair cracked surfaces with filler or consider replastering or skimming. Some interiors, usually country properties with stone walls, may have rough plastered walls, which enhance and complement the structure, and these should be retained, if possible. Doors, door frames, skirting boards, window frames and picture and dado rails are normally decorated in a more hard-wearing solvent-based paint. To minimize any unpleasant paint fumes, increase the drying times. Water-based paints have been developed in eggshell and satin finishes, as well as gloss, which will make application easier and fumes less noticeable.

surfaces

paint types

paint colours

stencilling

wallpaper

walls

Surfaces

Whatever your wall surface, the effect will be simplest if most of the walls are treated in the same way. That doesn't mean colour, texture or materials are forbidden. Plain plaster walls will blend, exposed brick looks dramatic and panelling adds elegance.

Plaster in a smooth, painted finish is the surface most people opt for. Rough, damaged or textured walls can be skimmed with a thin coat of plaster by a professional to give an even surface. The true character of stone-built properties will be retained if the walls are of rough-rendered, unrestored plaster, particularly those revealing an attractive patinated or painted finish, which can be sealed with a matt acrylic varnish for cleaning.

Tiles are eminently practical in kitchens and bathrooms, where they provide a waterproof, easy-clean surface. Ceramic tiles are available in an ever-widening range of finishes, including stone and slate, and stainless-steel tiles can also be found (see pages 186–7).

Panelling is usually part of the original architecture and helps to form the character of a house. In a simple interior, the detailing will stand out without the need to highlight it in a different colour. If a wall is uneven, or there is a noise or damp problem, installing plain panelling can be a solution.

Tongue-and-groove gives a country-style feel and is useful for covering up an uneven or unsightly wall finish. It is readily available in narrow 'matchstick' boards from home-decorating stores, but wider widths can be custom-made to create a more sophisticated look.

'Raw finishes', such as exposed brick, concrete and bare plaster, are simple and fashionable. They are, however, prone to dust and will need sealing. Several products give a clear invisible coating, but get advice as some sealants result in an unnatural, shiny appearance.

Paint types

Each of the different paint ranges on the market has its own specific look and suitability for use. Generally, emulsion paints and distempers are used for walls and are essentially water-based. Gloss and eggshell finishes are applied to woodwork and are frequently solvent-based, though water-based versions are now available. Specialist companies have adapted the content of their paints to minimize any detrimental effects on the environment and health.

Emulsion is a standard finish for walls. It is an easy-to-apply water-based paint, available in a huge range of colours, many of which can be mixed to your precise specifications. Modern emulsions cover well, sometimes with just one coat, and can be wiped clean. They can be applied to most cleaned and prepared sound surfaces, including bare plaster, wallpaper, old paint, brick, stone and wood. Spray-painting is a useful method for covering textured surfaces.

Distemper consists of pigments and binders, such as glues and natural resins, dispersed in water. If you have detailed mouldings, which would become clogged and lose definition with the application of emulsion paint, distemper is a good choice. However, it must be used correctly in order to achieve an even finish. The product is unstable if applied too thickly and should be applied with a brush; alternatively, use a spray for fragile plasterwork or brickwork.

To achieve a good depth of colour, several coats of paint may be required. It should be thinned down according to the porosity of the surface to which it is being applied. Bare plaster will require several thin coats, but distemper can also be applied on top of emulsion. Due to the nature of its composition, distemper will rub off easily and cannot be cleaned. This makes it unsuitable for areas of high wear, such as staircases or children's rooms.

Woodwork paints create a hard-wearing coating that preserves and protects wood surfaces. Windows, door frames and skirting boards are susceptible to scuffing and finger marks, and window frames are vulnerable to condensation. Traditionally, solvent- and oil-based gloss paints have been used as they form a hard, water-resistant coating, but they are also difficult to apply and care must be taken to ensure a smooth surface.

Water-based versions, including gloss, eggshell and some new flat finishes, have been developed and these are safer for the environment and your own health. Gloss looks fresh and clean, reflects the light and highlights woodwork. Eggshell has a soft sheen that creates a more subtle look. The new flat finishes are low-sheen or matt, which enables them to blend with

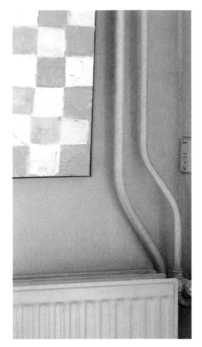

emulsion paint

wallpaper

gloss paint

the walls and gives a wonderfully restrained look to a room, but they are not recommended for kitchens or bathrooms.

Paint colours

An interest in 'heritage' styles, along with the demand for ever-more subtle finishes, has led to a number of specialist paint companies developing ranges that reproduce the shades and softer finishes of past eras. Collections made for major paint companies by well-known designers are also available. These tend to focus on the latest trends and often include useful categories, such as whites and neutrals. Many of the large commercial companies have redefined their colour choices and offer ranges that are based on moods, as well as historical and architectural styles.

Wherever you buy your paint, you will already be aware that white is no longer just white. There

are numerous versions, from the blue brightness of 'brilliant' white to the greige tints of lime-white. Brilliant white is the most inexpensive and it dominates the shelves of large home-decorating stores. As it contains blue, it can look cold and harsh, and may also be unflattering to the space and its contents. It is a little unforgiving too, as it highlights imperfections and can make perfectly clean items look dirty.

Look for plain white, which is softer and not as costly as special blended whites. It may not be sold in large, economic quantities, but it can often be found in builders' merchants at trade prices and in trade quality (which tends to be slightly thicker for better coverage).

Neutrals include the darker shades of white as well as soft tones of grey, beige, grey-green and light brown, which correspond to the colours of wood, stone, natural fibres and pale foliage.

Stencilling

Although considered a more ornate form of wall decoration, stencilling can also be used in a restrained, simple way. Limiting the palette can ensure continuity throughout a home, while introducing a subtle pattern as variation. As with paint effects, use colours that are similar in tone or character. Some of the historic paint collections share a similar quality even when the colours are quite different, and will all work well together.

Wallpaper

Wallpaper is back in fashion, but the modern approach is to use it in a more limited way. Apply a decorative wallpaper on just one wall for use as a feature or use it in a small room where the rest of the contents are low key or similar in style, colour or material. The newest ranges of wallpaper combine large-scale patterns with more subtle colourings.

Windows

Plain, uncomplicated curtains, blinds or shutters, or no window coverings at all, are an important feature of a simple-looking interior. Ornate headings and pelmets have been replaced by plain poles, rods, wires and ungathered curtains, hung on metal curtain rings, threaded through large eyelets or attached to clip-on fittings. If you are fortunate enough to have beautiful, well-proportioned windows, and the benefit of privacy and a pleasant view, leave the windows unadorned. Alternatively, shutters, blinds, simple panels and plain curtains can cover or disguise unsightly windows and minimize their impact. Small window proportions can be altered in emphasis by using full-length curtains, translucent panels or shutters to give the illusion of taller windows. Lined curtains may be vital to keep out draughts and, in townhouses, to filter the dust and grime of city streets. Window coverings filter and regulate the light, which can substantially change the mood of a space. Consider the aspect and function of the room; for example, covered windows at night give a warmer, more intimate feel.

curtains

fixtures

blinds

windows

Curtains

Various fabrics and lengths of curtain can be used in an interior, depending on your lighting and draught-proofing requirements, as well as the proportions and style of the space. Experiment with a sheet draped over a curtain pole to see how different lengths work together with your window and space proportions. Hemming curtains midway between the window-sill and the floor gives a more modern 'floating' effect and this works particularly well with high ceilings.

An interior that responds to seasonal changes allows for the welcome light of spring and summer, and the chillier autumn and winter evenings. In the winter months, heavier curtains can be substituted for lightweight versions. Long panels in heavy felted wool that skim the floor will form an efficient draught excluder.

While heavier weights of fabric, such as wool or flannel, add warmth, lightweight voile, muslin, plain cottons and linens create a fresh summery feel. Plain colours allow the curtains to blend in with the walls, but this is not the only option – a pale damask or hessian fabric can provide a little textural relief in an otherwise stark space.

Panels are the simplest form of window covering. Hemmed lengths of ungathered fabric can be fixed at the top with ties, eyelets or rings, or threaded onto a slim pole or wire. Wide panels can be used as conventional curtains, pulled back to either side when more light is required. Translucent panels, either alone or combined with heavier curtains, make an ideal permanent covering by allowing light diffusion and extra privacy.

Panels are easy to make, but most home-decorating shops and departments now sell an excellent range of ready-made versions. Alternatively, buy conventional curtains in the same width as the window and don't gather them.

Ready-made curtains in plain fabrics are extremely good value. Many are made with tabbed tops, ties, simple casings or eyelets. Others have traditional taped headings with hooks, but these can be used ungathered and hung from rings on less conventional fittings, such as tension wire or a galvanized pole.

Double curtains provide additional insulation during the chillier months of the year. Rather than changing

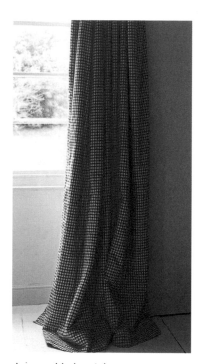

long padded curtains

the curtains at the onset of cooler weather, simply add a thicker curtain behind the summer covering using a length of Velcro to secure it in place. This method provides a cleaner look than a double curtain-track system and maintains the style of the more lightweight fabric.

Padded curtains are another option for conserving heat. Padding lightweight fabric with wadding can keep out draughts.

Wadding in varying thicknesses can be inserted between two fabric layers to create a reversible padded curtain.

Fixtures

Plain metal poles or wires create a streamlined effect that looks stylish when paired with curtain panels in unlined plain fabrics. However, there are many other forms of fixtures that can blend into the walls or be concealed. Avoid complicated tracking systems, as they can look obvious and overbearing. Heavy weights of fabric can be hung on more discreet tracking systems or on simple metal poles.

More decorative fixtures, such as clip-on rings or poles in modern shapes, can be used as a feature. These work best if they link with other hardware in the space; for example, by using aluminium fixings in a room where the door handles and furniture legs are also aluminium.

Buying all the fixtures separately is often possible, and as the sizes tend to be standard, you can mix and match them. Using wooden poles with simple metal fixings and rings will look lighter and fresher than traditional wooden fittings.

Poles in a range of metal finishes, most with shaped finials, can be bought in department stores and interiors shops. High street stores now have excellent ranges of poles, simple fittings and rings in stainless steel, as well as galvanized and dull metal finishes. Lengths of metal rod, including galvanized piping, used as reinforcing rods or for plumbing, can be found in builders'

merchants and home-decorating stores. Buying this way is not only cheaper, but also avoids the extra cost of unwanted decorative finials and brackets, which are often included in ready-packaged systems. In addition, the range of brackets and fixings for pipework is plain, practical and simple. Steel engineering rods, available from architectural and ironmongery wholesalers, have an attractive, minimalist look.

Wooden poles provide an alternative, but buy them without finials on the ends. If you own thick, old-fashioned wooden poles, these can be easily painted to merge with the background.

Curtain wire systems were initially devised using techniques and materials available in hardware shops and builders' suppliers. Now available from high street decorating shops, they have been adapted for ease of use and they look more sophisticated, often containing stainless-steel components. As with metal curtain poles, modern systems include all fittings and rings.

Curtain track has improved and systems now incorporate discreet metal strips and fixings that can be used for curtains and panels, as well as for more rigid materials for blinds. Several sophisticated systems use stainless-steel rods and brackets, available in different finishes. Although expensive, they are beautifully designed.

Curtain rings can look clean and simple when sewn onto plain, ungathered curtains. Look for fine iron and steel, rather than brass or

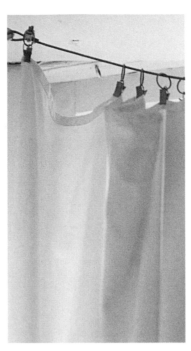

clip-on rings

old-fashioned wooden rings, and thread the rings onto slim metal rods. Several variations on curtain rings now exist, including metal rings with a loop for hooks.

Clip-on rings have a metal attachment that clips onto the curtain fabric without the need for tape or hooks. They can be bought in plain or decorative styles in a range of different finishes. Choose lightweight versions for thinner voile or muslin fabrics and more robust clips for heavier cottons and linens.

Eyelets are a tidy and streamlined way of hanging curtains as they avoid the need for hooks or rings and enable the curtain to slide effortlessly through poles. Large versions are available for hanging heavier weights of fabric. Eyelets work well on close weaves of fabric, such as linen, thick cotton or felted wool. Try to match the

eyelets

eyelet finish to the pole finish and make sure that the eyelet used is the correct size for the pole.

Eyelets are usually sold in kits, which include the tools for cutting and securing them. Space according to the weight of fabric – heavier curtains will require more closely spaced eyelets. Do not insert the eyelets too near the top edge of the curtain as the weight of the curtain may cause the fabric to pull away from the eyelets.

Blinds

Blinds maintain a clean look, whether they are efficient venetian blinds or soft gauze roman blinds. They use a minimal amount of fabric and can be drawn up into simple pleats. As blinds are usually fitted to the size of the window, and hung within the recess, they leave the walls free of fabrics and fittings, and can lighten the feel of a room. When constructed in a material that matches the walls,

windows

they will blend into the background when closed. They can be used to disguise less attractive windows or serve as a discreet presence on beautiful ones.

Blinds are adaptable; they can filter the light or even block it out, providing subtle light control as well as forming a convenient screen. Many types are available ready-made. Wood, metal, paper, fibre, bamboo, reed and plastic, as well as various cloth materials, complement different interior styles and can be chosen to suit the function of the space.

Roller blinds are the neatest and plainest form of blind. They can look formal in stiffened fabric and almost invisible when made from muslin. Rolled up, roller blinds are barely noticeable and will not interfere with the light or impinge on an uncluttered space. They look best when secured to the inside of a window frame, but blinds can also be hung over the top of the window if the fixing is not straightforward.

Kits consisting of a pole and cord mechanism can be bought for making your own blinds. A soft, unstructured look may be created by attaching a length of lightweight fabric in the correct width to the roller using adhesive or hook-and-loop tape fastener. Ready-made roller blinds, including blackout and water-resistant versions, can be bought in various widths and may be cut to fit.

A recent development are paper roller blinds, which look fresh and modern. The surface of the paper has small cut-outs, which add texture and create interesting light and shadow effects.

woollen roman blind

translucent linen roman blind

Roman blinds incorporate wooden battens, which enable them to form neat pleats when the blind is pulled up by the cords. Thick cottons and natural linens are ideal fabric choices for these traditional types of blind. A less formal style, without battens, looks softer.

Lightweight translucent fabrics will filter the light and are ideal in summer or for spaces that don't need to be draught-proof or light-proof. Blinds that are slightly wider and longer than the windows can be cosy and efficient, especially if made in heavier fabrics, such as woollen flannels or lined cotton. They can be lined with blackout or draught-excluding fabric.

Although relatively simple to make, especially the more unstructured styles, ready-made versions are available in a variety of widths, lengths and materials. To maintain a simple look, avoid any with scalloped or other decorative edges.

Venetian blinds were once expensive, often had to be made to measure and were considered difficult to keep clean. Their hard-edged look was associated with offices rather than domestic interiors. However, they are now appreciated for their clean lines, which complement modern spaces and warehouse-style lofts.

Wood looks softer and warmer than metal blinds and will blend with most interiors. Dark wood can be dramatic, but may look heavy if used in small spaces or on small windows. Pale or paint-washed wood will be less dominant and allow more light to enter the room. Thickness and depth of slats varies, so choose thinner, narrower versions for a more subtle look. As some of the blind will always be seen, consider where you place it. For example, venetian blinds would not be practical on casement windows or French doors where you need frequent access.

fabric shutters

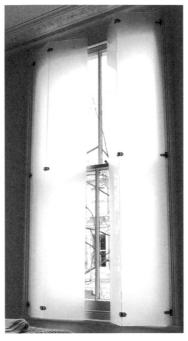
Perspex shutters

Wooden blinds look better if they are left down permanently, providing a gentle form of light control when open and an efficient blackout at night.

Metal venetian blinds can have very thin and narrow slats, which make them less obtrusive than wood. Available to order in a large range of colours, they are widely available in standard widths in white and silver. They look cool and sophisticated, especially when incorporated into the design of the interior, but can appear cold and clinical, if used with lots of hard edges and expanses of white. Metal blinds can be highly effective on large glass windows, where they can be adjusted to open up or close off views.

Natural fibre blinds, made from such materials as reed, bamboo and paper, are inexpensive and add a definite textural effect. Their simple structure and mechanisms often make them easy to cut to the correct width.

Used as a permanent window covering, they soften the look of an interior and can screen any unattractive views. The different materials vary in their translucency; although all will provide a degree of privacy during daylight, some become transparent when the lights are on at night. Pleated paper and fibre blinds are usually fairly opaque, but may look a little heavy, if left down during the day.

Shutters

Shutters can complement or emphasize beautiful, well-proportioned windows and disguise or cover up less attractive styles. The ones that fold away completely allow tall, elegant windows to be displayed. Double shutters are particularly useful as the top section can be left open to let in light, while the bottom serves as a screen for privacy. An illusion of a floor-length window can be created by placing full-length double shutters across an ordinary window and just opening the top.

Traditionally, shutters fit inside the window frame, but if your frames are metal or fit flush with the wall, or you wish to cover the whole window, then the shutters can be fixed outside the frame. Not all windows are suitable for shutters. Check the frame to work out where hinges can be attached and to see if there is space for folding back the shutters. Work out every aspect of how the shutter will open and close.

To ensure that the shutter can be moved through 180 degrees, strips or small blocks of wood may need to be fixed to the wall so that the hinges are level with the frame edge. Double hinges will enable panels to fold back on themselves. Builders' merchants and home-decorating shops can offer advice on the best hinge for your window.

Wood, naturally finished or painted, is the most frequently used material for shutters, though Perspex, medium-density fibreboard (MDF) and plywood are also suitable. Plain, painted MDF or plywood panels are cost-effective and relatively easy to install yourself. Several companies offer made-to-measure louvre-style versions. For more sophisticated designs involving panels, or for homes that are architecturally distinctive, employ a professional carpenter to custom-make and install the shutters.

Translucent acrylic sheeting, such as Perspex, filters the light beautifully and looks modern, yet delicate. A relatively expensive material, acrylic needs to be cut carefully to avoid cracking and the edges must be smoothed down without damaging the surface. Acrylic scratches easily, so avoid using it in areas where it may be subjected to rough treatment. You will need extra sets of hinges to ensure that this slightly flexible material will not warp. Unless you can buy ready-finished pieces, have them professionally made.

Lightweight fabric may be hung on a narrow frame or slender metal rods, see far left, and secured with simple screw hooks or eyes. It combines the practicality and visual impact of a shutter with the translucence of a muslin or gauze.

Screens

Using screens in front of a window can provide privacy while leaving the windows bare and uncluttered by curtains or blinds. They may be easily moved, or removed, to suit different times of day or changing seasons. The newest versions are made from translucent materials, including paper, gauze and acrylic sheet. Paper screens in a wooden frame give a crisp feel to a room. The traditional folding screen is flexible and adaptable, but there are also sculptural, curved shapes available in card, paper, slatted wood and lightweight plastics.

Simple screens can be made from lengths of wood or medium-density fibreboard (MDF), joined with hinges. Old screens may be found in junk shops and antique markets. Look out for old hospital-style screens on wheels, which can easily be rejuvenated with a coat of paint and some new fabric.

Heating

The type of heating you choose depends on where you live and what is available and practical for your home. But the impact of heating systems and sources on interiors cannot be ignored – an open fire may provide a welcome focus, but unsightly appliances can create an irritating distraction. If you are able to replace an old heating system, then you can choose one that is suited to both your home and style of interior. Warm air and under-floor heating systems offer the least intrusive method, leaving you free to place furniture and fittings without too many restrictions. They are usually installed when the house is built, but can be incorporated into new building works. It is worth considering installing an under-floor system if you are having a new floor laid; a concrete or wood floor works particularly well with this form of heating.

Radiators will be visible and any scheme needs to incorporate visually pleasing ones, or to disguise or screen unattractive units. Fireplaces provide a wonderful focus for a room and create an aura of warmth, with or without a real fire burning. Stoves, whether inherited with the home or newly installed, are similarly comforting and can also be a source of heating. Their shape and size can turn them into a sculptural presence or part of the architecture of the space. Before undertaking any renovation of a fireplace or stove, or using one for the first time, consult a chimney sweep or home-heating expert who can make the necessary safety checks.

radiators

fireplaces

gas fires

stoves

tall modern radiators

cast-iron radiators

industrial radiators

Radiators

Modern radiators are attractive and an efficient method of heating. Smaller sizes can now heat larger spaces, while requiring less wall space. The variety of types and choice of materials and colours is such that it is possible to find designs that suit the style and character of any property. Making radiators as discreet as possible has always been paramount, but the availability of new shapes and finishes offers the chance to use them as a feature. Plain, flat panels or radiator covers, painted in the same colour as the wall, will be barely noticeable. Placing tall slim radiators behind doors maximizes otherwise unusable space and keeps the rest of the wall clear. Low, floor-level radiators also have minimal impact.

Traditional cast-iron radiators, found in old houses, schools and office buildings, are currently popular. Their generous proportions and industrial style are well suited to large rooms, lofts, warehouse-style dwellings and older properties. Re-conditioned old radiators can be found in architectural salvage yards and several manufacturers have now added retro styles to their ranges.

Modern and distinctive designs are produced by specialized radiator manufacturers. Dramatic spirals, curves and grids, from long and low shapes to tall and slim, can be used in selected areas, such as bathrooms, where they provide a unique focal point. As they can be a dramatic presence, use them as a one-off feature in a minimal space.

Electric radiators are independent units fitted with timers and plugs. They are more efficient and less energy-consuming than they once were. Mobile types can be hidden out of sight in warmer weather.

minimal fireplace

traditional fire surround

Fireplaces

If you wish to open up and use a previously boarded-up fireplace, note that there are strict rules and regulations, especially in towns, relating to pollution and health and safety. Before carrying out any changes, consult a chimney sweep, builder or expert and check with your local authority on any possible restrictions on the use of fuel. A good chimney sweep can advise you on the state and efficiency of your chimney, and will be able to point out any possible negative consequences of changes you wish to make.

A newly opened-up fireplace with an exposed brick back and hearth looks attractive and it may be possible to use it in this raw state. However, the brickwork of the chimney can be damaged if the fire bricks are not replaced, so consult an expert for advice on the requirements of the hearth. A raised hearth may be constructed using bricks, but the shape and construction of the chimney can limit where you place the fire.

You may wish to adapt, change the style or raise the level to create a recessed fireplace, without a mantelpiece or hearth to spoil the minimal lines, as above left.

Fire surrounds, particularly old-fashioned ones, can be removed and replaced with simpler, more elegant designs. Removing an old surround, and taking out the fireback and grate, is not usually difficult. However, the grate may be sealed to the fireback with asbestos, a hazardous material that must be handled and disposed of by a professional.

Traditional fire surrounds and mantelpieces with graceful curves and proportions will enhance many styles of interior, especially if they are stripped of any ornate detailing or tiles. Architectural salvage companies and antique shops stock a variety of fire surrounds in different shapes and sizes and in marble, stone, wood and metal. Specialist companies sell both re-conditioned and new fireplaces, some in attractive, plain styles. Carpenters or joiners can build you a simple shape in wood, which can then be painted or finished.

Gas fires

Gas fires are a cleaner alternative to solid fuel and eliminate the disadvantages of dust and mess. Coal-effect styles can look convincing without being ornate or artificial-looking. Several new, innovative designs include simple stone bowls filled with flaming pebbles and dramatic sculptural shapes incorporating real flames. For these types, a chimney is needed and a flue liner may be required to avoid the build-up of harmful gases.

Stringent regulations apply to gas-fuelled fires and installation must be carried out by a registered installer. In the UK they need to be registered with the Council of Registered Gas Installers (CORGI).

Stoves

Wood-burning and other solid fuel stoves are efficient sources of heat and some can also heat water. Clean and contained, they have the feel of a real fire, but are much safer. Their simple, ergonomic shapes can look stylish, especially in matt black or stainless-steel finishes. Scandinavian stoves are sought after for their modern and well-designed look.

In the absence of a chimney, connecting stoves to a balanced flue placed on an outside wall may be possible, but you will need expert advice and installation.

Lighting

Lighting has an enormous influence on an interior and can completely change the ambience of a space, from bright efficiency to subdued intimacy or anywhere in between. It is a huge topic, with a wide choice of styles and categories according to types of lighting for specific purposes and levels of illumination. Start with good, general lighting, then use individual lamps to create different moods and highlight specific areas or objects. Floor-standing, table and desk lights can be moved, so changing their effect is easily achieved. Installing dimmer switches allows the light intensity to be precisely adjusted. Simple lighting solutions can mix the practical, sophisticated and understated, while also injecting occasional touches of flamboyance and romanticism.

The industrial look, with its honest use of materials and simple construction, is perfect for large spaces and pared-down interiors. Work lamps, especially the clip-on variety, are adaptable and usually inexpensive, and the angled desk lamp can be used in many locations unconnected with work. Old light fittings rescued from factories and offices may be found in salvage yards, antique shops and even skips and junk yards. An unusual table lamp can inject character into a minimal space or become a striking stand-alone feature. Large ranges of modern, beautifully designed lamps, light fittings and complete systems may be found in interiors shops, as well as specialist retailers, some of which also stock classic 20th-century designs. The increased demand for good, modern style means that even high street shops offer suitable contemporary lighting, often at remarkably low prices.

overhead

concealed

wall

work

table and
floor

Overhead lighting

General overhead lighting, fixed to the ceiling, is used for areas where high light levels are required, such as kitchens, bathrooms, work spaces and staircases. A single central light is now considered unfashionable, as it casts a harsh light over the whole area, but fitting dimmer switches will enable greater light control.

Downlighters, normally set into the ceiling, will give good general light, and this unobtrusive form has replaced tracks of spotlights as the favoured light source in kitchens. Setting them near the edges of a room, so that the light 'washes' down the wall, produces a more subtle effect. Downlighters are somewhat complicated to fit as they need to be set into the ceiling void; consequently, they may be unsuitable for certain properties.

Overhead spotlights throw good directional light onto working areas and can be angled upwards for a wash of light. Long tracks with several spotlights are not as fashionable as they once were, but smaller groups of up to four bulbs, fixed onto a short track or central round plate, are now available in a whole range of styles and finishes, including white, aluminium, stainless steel and brushed steel.

Independent shaped bulbs or spotlights can look stylish when hung on long cables, either singly or in rows. The bulbs may be moved along the cable to suit your requirements. They look good in both modern and old properties.

A number of beautifully designed, highly sophisticated spotlight systems can also be purchased. Normally specified by architects and interior designers, they involve tracking systems and offer high levels of light control. They are more costly and will need professional installation.

Pendant lights are set low to throw a pool of concentrated, more controlled, light over an area. There are no fixed rules for the height of pendant lights – it depends on the style and function of the piece. Some versions have a rise-and-fall mechanism, so the height can be easily adjusted. However, if you are using pendant lights over a table, make sure that the bulb won't shine uncomfortably into your eyes when you are seated, and that you will not bang your head when sitting down or reaching for food.

Glass, plastic or paper shades will diffuse the light, as well as direct it, whereas metal or other opaque materials throw all the light downwards. Large utilitarian aluminium shades are a good choice for simple, spacious rooms.

Chandeliers can provide a little light relief to sparse settings. A simple interior does not mean a severe one, and an unashamedly pretty chandelier can provide an elegant focal point. Sculptural or modern forms will introduce curved shapes to a hard-edged interior, traditional delicate crystal versions look romantic, and unique quirky finds can add character.

naked bulb in a ceramic socket

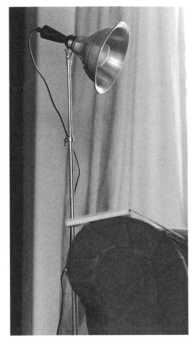
work lamp

pendant light

angled desk lamp

Concealed lighting

With concealed lighting, there are no visible fixtures and fittings to spoil the clean lines of an interior. The light source is normally set behind discreet panels at ceiling or floor height, but sophisticated versions are incorporated into the interior design at the planning stage. Concealed lighting can be created by installing a panel in front of a row of downlighters, spotlights or a striplight, but check the safety recommendations to ensure that the panel does not become a fire hazard.

Concealed lights beneath kitchen units provide good worktop lighting without illuminating the whole space. They are usually incorporated into the kitchen design and installed with fitted units, but simple plug-in versions can be bought to fit under cupboards or shelves.

A variety of recessed and concealed lighting has been specifically designed for bathroom use. Many systems provide good lighting for mirrors, but will need installation by an electrician, as all wiring needs to be kept away from water sources and switches must be pull-cords or located outside the bathroom.

Wall lights

Wall lights give a soft form of light and are frequently used in kitchens and bathrooms, where they are functional rather than decorative. When used above worktops, sinks and basins, they are neat and understated, but give out plenty of diffused light. The plainest types are circular ceramic lights that can be attached to the wall. Bulkhead lights are contained, waterproof units that may be used outdoors and in bathrooms. With their wire protective covering, they look functional, but more sophisticated versions feature etched glass with narrow, stainless-steel rims.

Work lamps

Work lights suit a pared-down architectural interior, but also combine surprisingly well with more traditional styles of home. Old office and factory lights from the 1940s and '50s, in iron or steel, often have beautiful shapes and a worn, industrial look. A single spotlight, fixed to the wall or clipped onto a shelf, makes a perfect reading light or can highlight a favourite picture.

Angled desk lamps are adjustable, stylish and functional. Their timeless and versatile design makes them ideal for table, bedside and floor lighting. Standard versions are affordable; classic designs can be expensive, but are made of high-quality materials and are beautiful, so often well worth the investment.

Photography and film industry lighting equipment has been adapted for the domestic market. The simplest feature aluminium shades and clip-on fittings, and are often called loft lights. As these lights are equipped with a plug, they can be attached to shelves and headboards, or to metal stands to transform them into floor lights. Loft lights are available in sophisticated designs and in high-quality materials; look for glass and colour finishes.

Table and floor lights

Table and floor lamps give a subtle light that creates a more subdued and cosy ambience. Shapes and styles vary from the traditional lamp base with a paper shade to minimalist metal stems topped with glass shades. Paper lamps provide a soft glow, while curvaceous, retro-style lamps add character. Don't be afraid to use a decorative or colourful lamp; it will add a personal touch and temper any cold or stark effects.

Kitchens

The kitchen has evolved from being a place for preparing and cooking food to the centre of social activity. Like any room in the home, it exhibits the personality of its inhabitants. Some kitchens are disciplined and minimal; others show evidence of family life or a love of cooking and entertaining. A continuity of materials and colour will maintain a clean-looking background for an area that has to accommodate and serve a number of needs, from food preparation and storage to washing up.

The choice of kitchen styles is diverse and ever-expanding. Personal taste, lifestyle, the shape and size of the space, compatibility with the character of the property and available budget are among the many factors to be considered. The influence of restaurant style is apparent in many contemporary domestic kitchens. Catering-style kitchens, with their industrial-size cookers, large expanses of worktop and large sinks, look efficient and businesslike. Wood and natural stone look warm, yet practical, while concrete and stainless steel are cool and streamlined. To keep the look simple, choose restrained designs and plain cupboards and shelves – don't be tempted by such add-ons as decorative plate racks or carved detailings and mouldings. Use a material that will last and mature with age, rather than show wear or chip. If possible, spend a little extra to achieve timelessness and quality. That said, inexpensive can be chic. Replacing handles and work surfaces with more high-grade materials makes cheap kitchen units look smarter, and a medley of styles can be united under a single worktop.

fitted

unfitted

catering

work benches

surfaces

kitchens

Fitted

The benefit of fitted kitchens is that they are tailored to suit the space and your requirements, and their uniformity creates a simple background. A wide choice of base units, drawers, cupboards, shelves and appliance cabinets can be put together in an almost unlimited variety of ways.

Help with planning is usually available from the suppliers, but make sure you have some idea of how it will look in elevation – combinations that work well on a plan may not work in reality. When planning wall cupboards and fixtures, remember to keep them in line with the base units to ensure they look balanced. Cost depends on quality, choice of materials and style, but employing a professional to fit the kitchen is worth the financial outlay.

Unfitted

Unfitted kitchens are highly fashionable and they appear more solid than fitted kitchens, as each element is free-standing and a piece of furniture rather than a 'unit'. The pieces are usually wider and longer than standard units, and include full-height storage and island work stations.

Not having to fix them to the wall is an advantage, especially if your walls are unsuitable or uneven. They are best positioned so that there is space around each piece.

Mixing styles is possible with unfitted units. A collection of storage items can work well together, even if they are of different materials and styles. Ideally the pieces should be good quality, functional or very beautiful. Antique, retro and industrial designs can add character and charm. Consider unconventional pieces, too. School, hospital and office furniture and equipment is often very suitable, generous in size and generally well made. Consider the 'alternative use' of pieces. For example, old pigeonholes or a row of lockers can serve as storage and an old slate slab may become a worktop.

oak and steel drawers

Catering styles

Now that restaurant kitchens are as stylish as restaurants, the professional catering style has spread to domestic interiors. The generous proportions, clean lines, shiny surfaces and industrial detailing are very much in tune with modern design. Look at professional catering suppliers – many of them sell to the domestic market. Most units are free-standing and can be placed in a number of positions. Stainless-steel sink units and work benches can be found. The sizes are large, so you may need a big space to fully explore this approach.

Work benches

A work bench or island, where sink, hob, storage and worktop are combined in one unit, looks compact and streamlined. It can be placed in less-conventional areas, such as the centre of the room. The most extravagant are sleek, stainless-steel versions on slender legs.

Surfaces

The available variety and quality of kitchen materials has increased enormously in recent years. Choice of work surface depends on a combination of aesthetic, practical and cost factors. To keep a simple look, choose a material that matches or complements the floor or the fittings.

Materials such as wood, stone, slate, terrazzo, concrete, metal and an ever-increasing range of composites and laminates are widely available. A number of flooring materials can also be used for worktops (see page 187). Wood and stone surfaces will need initial treatments and regular maintenance to keep them in good condition and many will develop an attractive patina with regular use. Laminates are easy to clean, and hard finishes, such as terrazzo, ceramic tiles and polished granite, are highly practical. Stainless steel is popular, with zinc, concrete and rubber being newer alternatives. Reclaimed wood, marble and slate slabs add character and a warm 'living' quality that works well with hard-edged modern fittings.

white and concrete fitted units

simple unfitted kitchen

All work surfaces are prone to wear, and can become stained and damaged through use. Take basic precautions by using chopping boards to protect against the inevitable scratches and stains, and trivets to avoid burns.

Some of the materials listed below can also be used for splashbacks. Tiles give a clean, professional look and will blend with most kitchen designs. Stainless-steel sheeting looks modern and stylish. Stone gives a softer, more expensive and luxurious look. Using the same material for the worktop and the splashback will help to unify non-matching storage and appliances.

Laminates are readily available, relatively inexpensive and easy to use. Composed of a hard layer of synthetic material that is laminated

to a reconstituted wood base, they are easy to cut and fit, and are ideal for the preparation of food and general kitchen use. Available in different colours, finishes and textures, including metallic, stone and wood effects, they provide an effective way to unite a group of unrelated units. If selected in the same colour as the units and walls, laminates will blend easily into the background.

Wood gives a warm and mellow look to a kitchen. It enhances the style of old and traditional houses, can add character to new spaces and softens the hard lines and materials of metal appliances and modern units. Solid wood should be used and a dense grain is more efficient and hard-wearing. Beech, maple and oak will need to be treated, usually with boiled

linseed oil, but teak has natural oils and requires less frequent oiling. Sealing the wood helps to provide an easy-care, stain-resistant surface, but allowing this natural material to breathe and look after itself will enable it to develop an attractive, mature appearance (see also page 185).

Stone is another natural material that can look good in almost any style of interior. Slate and granite, with their dark colouring and hard surfaces, are perfect for worktops, but limestone is now frequently used to give a lighter, softer look (see also page 187). After an initial treatment to reduce the porosity, limestone will stay clean with regular wiping down and, as with floors, will develop an attractive patina and eventually look after itself. Care must be taken to avoid

kitchens

contact with lemon juice, which 'burns' into the surface, leaving stains that defy removal.

Concrete worktops are usually cast on site. To be robust and hygienic, the mixture needs to be specially formulated and the surface will usually be polished to decrease the porosity.

Stainless steel has clean edges and a cool simplicity that will give a sharp, modern feel to a kitchen. It is a good functional material that is easy to clean, hygienic and highly light-reflective. A sink and worktop can be formed from a single sheet – with no seams or sharp edges, it looks smart and architectural.

Stainless steel does mark and can become slightly duller and scratched with use. Regular maintenance involving special polishes will maintain its new finish, but the more muted sheen that develops in time is also attractive. If you are a keen cook and like a kitchen to look well-used, you may appreciate this softer effect.

Zinc has a wonderful dull sheen that works well with wood and provides an unusual and more subtle alternative to shiny stainless steel. Manufactured in sheets, it is normally wrapped around the edges of a work surface. The surface will mark and stain if it is not treated, but the material forms a patina with use. A sealant is usually applied that will prevent excess damage, but a completely impervious coating gives an artificial, unnatural look.

Rubber is sometimes used as a work surface and is, in fact, highly

tiled splashbacks

marble work surface

practical. Used mainly in sheet form, it is inset into a metal or wooden surround. Resistant to heat and spills, and easy to clean, its matt finish and soft surface is sympathetic to most styles of kitchen, from the traditional to the very modern.

Composites, such as terrazzo, are formed from mixes of ground or powdered materials combined with pigments and bonding agents. The method of production produces a more consistent finish than natural materials and it has its own quality and character.

Available as tiles or slabs, composites can also be moulded into one-piece sink and worktop units. Many companies offer flooring in the same material and finish. Moulded composites have a smooth, matt finish and rounded edges. Chipping and cracking can be a problem, so commission an expert for advice and installation.

Tiles give an efficient and hard-edged look. Although not as suitable for worktops, they provide a waterproof, easy-to-clean surface for splashback areas. Tiles are available in both glazed and matt finishes (see also page 187).

Sinks

Sinks can be made in the conventional materials of porcelain and composites or plastic, but sourcing an old stone sink or custom-making a concrete surface will make your kitchen more unique. Composites and plastics are easy-care, but porcelain, stone and concrete will chip if heavy items are accidentally dropped or banged against them. They are also unforgiving to dropped china and glass, which will almost certainly break on contact.

Porcelain sinks, based on the traditional butler's sinks, have straight lines, a pure white colour and chunky good looks that make them perfect for a simple style approach. Some are fitted into a wooden surround with a draining board, but in these cases the sink loses its clean, stark shape. Standing them on large, sturdy metal brackets allows their shape to be enhanced, and placing them on wood or zinc plinths looks more unconventional. Other shapes that incorporate a drainage surface are available, as are luxurious versions made with a matt finish.

Stone sinks are beautiful but can be impractical, as items easily break on the surface. Antique, characterful sinks, like the chunky traditional French ones, can be found in architectural suppliers and salvage yards, and they have a wonderful patina of age. New stone sinks, often a single large bowl, impart a rustic look.

Concrete sinks, usually made on site, look good on their own or as part of a work surface. They seem modern when used with polished concrete floors and hard-edged materials and fittings, but also have a rugged appearance suited to less formal surroundings.

Stainless-steel sinks are practical, good-looking and come in a various permutations, from single round bowls to double sinks with integrated chopping boards. They look neat and simple when set into the worktop. New versions are smoothly moulded into seamless top units, incorporating a draining area, work surface and even splashbacks. Free-standing stainless-steel catering sinks can be surprisingly well-priced.

Plastic and composite sinks are popular as they are available in a range of colours and finishes. However, some are a little cheap-looking and over-detailed. Solid sinks moulded from composites can look stunning, especially when supported on a slender stainless-steel frame.

Taps

A mixer tap that swivels to serve two sinks is the most popular style for kitchens. The simplest designs look like laboratory taps – tall and slender, curving into a graceful arc. Some versions have a spray attachment, which is useful for rinsing vegetables as well as for washing dishes.

The choice between taps and levers depends on personal preference, though levers look smarter and will be easier for older, less nimble hands. Most taps are made from chrome-plated metal or stainless steel, with a choice of shiny or satin finish, but lacquered metal in a variety of colours is an alternative choice. High-tech modern taps do not need to be limited to minimal kitchens; they will contrast wonderfully with old styles and well-worn materials.

For old sinks that have two tap holes, you will need the traditional separate hot and cold taps. Look for old, reconditioned taps in a salvage yard or specialist retailer.

Appliances

Cookers, refrigerators, freezers, washing machines, dishwashers and microwaves are no longer necessarily white. Stainless steel has become a popular choice, as have combined units built into the

stainless-steel open unit

mix of styles

wall and island units. To keep a streamlined look, choose all the appliances in the same plain colour or finish, or hide them behind cupboard doors or relocate them to a larder or pantry. Alternatively, for refrigerators or cookers, make a bold statement with a free-standing retro style.

Built-in appliances, such as ovens, microwaves and hobs, allow greater flexibility in the use of space. Available in stainless steel and white or coloured enamel, they blend into a kitchen scheme and maintain a unified look.

Large industrial-style cookers and ranges can be found in most kitchen appliance centres. Their chunky shape suits the simple interior. New versions of old-fashioned enamelled ranges have become popular. However, they can look fussy, with too many knobs in shiny brass and

exaggerated decorative features, so look for the plainer versions.

Specialist companies sell re-conditioned stoves and ranges. There are strict rules regarding the sale of second-hand appliances, so make sure the seller has the correct paperwork to verify its suitability. If you acquire one from another source, arrange to have the cooker tested and approved as fit for use first.

Solid range cookers – such as the Aga – have timeless good looks and will fit in with most decors. They also heat water and can be used to run radiators. Some are expensive and very heavy, so you need to make sure the cooker can be installed in your home. Choose white or black from among the many colours on offer. These ranges usually become the heart of a home, a centre of warmth and comfort as well as a functional piece of equipment.

Bathrooms

For a simple style of bathroom, keep the surfaces practical and add touches of luxury or character. Function and efficiency are as important as appearance. The look should be pared-down without being cold or sterile. Many modern bathrooms have a 'bathhouse' feel, with tiled floors and walls that are suited to contact with water and steam. As with kitchens, the variety of materials and hardware has increased enormously in the last few years. Luxury finishes, such as marble and limestone, are now widely used for flooring, walls and baths and basins. For the inevitable splashing, choose surfaces and finishes that will not be damaged by contact with water.

Plain, white, porcelain butlers' sinks are popular for bathrooms as they have just the right look to fit in with traditional as well as contemporary settings. Modern designs for baths and sanitary fittings are streamlined, and many are produced specifically for small spaces. Small bathrooms can seem larger if they are efficient and plain, and their size may allow you to afford more expensive materials, fixtures and fittings. Antique or old-fashioned baths and basins are available and can be re-conditioned, but manufacturers also produce new versions based on old designs. Mixing styles is also possible – an old-fashioned bath can be placed alongside sleek, modern fittings or a stone bowl next to a state-of-the art shower. A bathroom is also a good place to indulge in the unexpected or to make a feature of a decorative surface, such as exuberant wallpaper or a marble floor. Consider your lifestyle when planning a bathroom; a pair of sinks to cope with rush-hours and family demands, or a separate shower cubicle in addition to a bath may be suitable options. Showers take up less space, but if you plan to eliminate a bath entirely, you may miss the opportunity for relaxed candle-lit bathing.

Basins

Basins and sanitary ware are available in porcelain, natural stones and composite materials. Glass basins and surrounds are best when plain, with bowls in clear or etched glass.

Some modern porcelain designs are elegant and streamlined, and there are ranges designed specifically for use in small spaces. For a simple style, choose a white colour. An attractive industrial look can be achieved by placing a butler's sink on heavy-duty metal brackets or supporting it on a wood, stone or distressed zinc plinth.

Limestone, marble and slate are frequently used for bathroom surfaces and basins. A slab of limestone, custom-cut in a narrow wedge, can become a stunning, minimal basin. Stone bowls look elemental and marble surrounds are practical as well as chic. Basins moulded from stone composites are seductively

smooth and can be obtained in several subtle colours.

Old and antique basins have their own elemental appeal and are much in demand. Look for well-worn marble basins and large porcelain basins or sinks with high splashbacks or exaggerated detailing. New basins can be given an old-fashioned look by setting them into a wooden surround or by supporting them on a metal or wooden frame, as seen right.

Baths

The old-fashioned bathtub on decorative feet is a timeless favourite. Look in salvage yards or specialist shops for genuine antiques. Many will have been re-enamelled, and the outsides may have been re-sprayed a colour. Stripping them down to the grey metal also looks good, but they will need to be sealed immediately with a clear lacquer to prevent rusting. The baths can also be bought unrestored and can be re-

basin on wooden frame

enamelled and resprayed, and the supplier may offer this service. If you have inherited an antique bath, the enamelling can be done in situ.

Manufacturers now reproduce some of the old shapes. Although they lack the character of the

bathrooms

genuine article, they have a new, enamelled surface and are made in a variety of standard sizes and colours. For a modern rather than a 'nostalgic' look, consider alternatives to the traditional feet, such as resting the bath on slabs of rough-hewn wood or stone.

Showers

Before installing a shower, ensure that the bathroom floor and any surrounding surfaces are leak- and waterproof. Avoid water splashing or seeping into areas where it may cause damage or staining to walls, floors and the ceilings below. Shower cabinets with glass doors can work well, but they may look obtrusive and may have corners and edges that are difficult to keep clean. Locating a shower in a recess or purpose-built space will keep splashes confined, and it may be possible to do without a shower curtain. Floor-to-ceiling tiles are an ideal waterproof surface (see page 190).

Shower curtains are a necessity for those with a shower over the bath. For maximum efficiency, make sure it is generous in length and width. Even the most expensive versions become stained in time and can be difficult to clean. Double curtains, such as a fabric or towelling curtain used with a separate waterproof liner, will hang better and can be laundered and changed frequently.

Taps

Even the most basic ranges of taps and showerheads include 'historic' styles, along with modern-looking designs, and they all have a choice of levers. Beautifully

porcelain sink on zinc

free-standing painted bath

double shower curtain

designed, luxury versions will enhance any style of bathroom and can make cheaper fittings look more expensive.

The choice of style will depend on personal taste and the design of the fittings, but don't be afraid to mix the clean lines and convenience of modern taps with traditional shapes or the less-than-perfect surfaces of old baths and basins. Taps that come straight out of the wall look stylish, especially when used above a minimal basin. As the pipework is concealed behind the wall or panel, the installation will be a little more complicated and they may be unsuitable for some bathrooms.

If you do want to use old taps, which have plenty of character, make sure they have been re-conditioned and work well. An old tap soon loses its charm if it leaks or is difficult to turn on and off. Whatever the style, invest in good quality, especially for showers.

Accessories

Storage and accessories, from toothbrush holders to large cabinets, are necessary requisites. Keep to simple essentials in the same style and material. Avoid getting carried away by providing a place for everything, as the result may look cluttered. Store items out of sight in a wall cabinet or display selected items neatly on shelves. Consider the details: blocks of soap look good in a wood or stone bowl, while plain hooks or pegs are useful for hanging towels.

Cupboards of some form are usually necessary in a bathroom, unless you have provided sufficient built-in units (see page 206). In a large bathroom, a wall-size cupboard can hold towels, soaps, toiletries, medicines and all the paraphernalia associated with health and hygiene in one place. Old medical cabinets and dental storage units add a functional

element and simple wooden, country-style cupboards can be repainted to work with the decor.

Radiators and towel rails are convenient for warmth and for drying towels. Take advantage of new designs, which include tall spirals and clear glass panels. They can look stunning and dramatic in a bathroom, whereas they may not fit in elsewhere in the home. Some radiators are designed to double as towel rails, and can run independently of the central heating system.

Linens and towels don't need to hang on heated rails. Instead, sew tags on them and hang them from simple hooks or wooden pegs. Bathmats are necessary on slippery floors, but put down simple woven cotton mats that can be washed easily. Alternatively, use wooden duckboarding, but this can be slippery when wet.

Storage

Storage plays an important role in the pursuit of clutter-free living. Even the most ardent non-materialist will have a surprising amount of possessions for which to find a place. Think big and don't be tempted by complicated storage systems and 'solutions'. Stowing items in one place or in one large piece of furniture is better than stashing smaller amounts in several locations or individual boxes, drawers and sundry containers. An entire room devoted to storage, such as a dressing room or pantry, can help keep other rooms more spacious and streamlined. A large, free-standing cupboard will hold a variety of objects and not only will they be easily accessible, but the cupboard itself can become an attractive feature of the interior.

Built-in storage is discreet, as well as efficient, particularly if the design is plain and there are no handles or knobs. A contrasting finish, such as dark wood, will add visual interest while still maintaining a united front. Fitted kitchen and bathroom units can be designed to incorporate ample storage for all the relevant equipment, but adding extra cupboards – perhaps covering an entire wall – will provide space for less frequently used items.

storage

Storage rooms

A whole room dedicated to storage may seem a luxury, but it will free up space in the rest of the interior and greatly enhance a simple, open look.

Under-used space in hallways, landings or below stairs can often be adapted, and better use can be made of larders or pantries. Converting a small room into a dressing room will leave the bedroom free of large furniture or fittings. A walk-in wardrobe, which does not need natural light, could be built into a bedroom space, or leading off from a bathroom.

Built-in storage

Made-to-measure storage keeps belongings out of sight behind closed doors and can be built to your specifications by a carpenter or specialist furniture company. Awkward or oddly-shaped spaces may be smoothed out and 'simplified' by adding built-in units. Storage can also be custom-made to house computers or entertainment centres.

A number of expensive, but extremely attractive, high-quality systems are now available in metal, etched glass and beautiful

free-standing cupboard

metal lockers

wood finishes. Self-assembly flat-pack systems are also suitable, as long as they are installed properly, but choose plain designs and substitute better-quality knobs and handles for those supplied.

Wall-size storage is a convenient way of maintaining order and units can be constructed to become virtually invisible, especially if magnetic or spring-loaded door closings are used instead of

knobs or handles. What appears to be a wood-panelled wall can actually be doors to storage cupboards, as in the bathroom pictured opposite, which houses clothes, towels and linens behind wall-to-wall cupboards. Built-in storage that is confined to one wall may take up a lot of space, but the overall effect will make the room look pared down and simple .

A wall of cupboards, built as a 'floating' or floor-to-ceiling partition, can be used to divide space and will keep all other walls clear. Concealing unsightly appliances behind a wall of doors will create order in a busy kitchen. Built-in wardrobes, with shelves, drawers, rails and racks specially designed for the purpose, will keep all clothes, shoes and accessories neatly out of sight.

Free-standing

Free-standing cupboards offer greater flexibility than built-in units, as you can rearrange them within a space and take them with you if you move home. They are ideal for storing large quantities of less-attractive necessities, including cooking utensils and food in a kitchen, files and a computer in an office, or tools and equipment in a work room. They will keep dust away from china and glassware, linens and clothes.

Used for tidying away toys and paperwork, cupboards will enable a space to be reclaimed or re-invented after the children have gone to bed or office work is finished for the day. Many new cupboards are designed specifically for the storage of modern-day accoutrements, such as video and music systems.

The scale and style of large cupboards can be incorporated into most interiors. Look for plain wardrobes fitted with shelves for capacious storage. Antique armoires and linen presses have character and charm, as well as plenty of space. A single beautiful or unusual cupboard can become the focal point of an interior. Country-style cupboards look good with original, worn paintwork, but can also be repainted.

Utility cabinets, such as old school, office, factory and hospital units, are usually large, well-made and reasonably priced, and they can be cleaned or stripped and repainted or polished. Medical cabinets are often metal with glass doors, making them particularly suitable for bathrooms. Hospital suppliers sell new ones, but old painted metal versions have lots of character and are robust. If the paintwork is unacceptably 'distressed', strip down to the bare metal and treat for rust or repaint.

Metal or wood lockers offer an unusual alternative. Find old ones from schools or institutions, or invest in new versions, which are available in a wide range of colours. Many companies that supply schools and leisure centres are happy to sell to individuals.

Chests of drawers may seem to be an obvious form of storage, but their attractiveness and efficiency are often overlooked in favour of more contemporary storage 'solutions'. Old and new versions are available in a variety of shapes, sizes and prices, and they can be used for items as diverse as papers and files, craft materials and clothing and accessories.

Containers

Lidded chests, trunks, boxes and baskets are excellent for long-term storage, such as blankets, bedlinens and off-season clothes. As well as being visually pleasing, simple styles of chests or trunks can supply additional opportunities for displaying objects or providing seating. Open baskets and boxes, perfect for toys and miscellaneous clutter, will work even better if fitted

wall of concealed cupboards

with castors so that they can be rolled away out of sight.

Containers in basketwork, Perspex or wood can provide tidy uniformed storage for regularly used items. Identical containers can be arranged in a series on window-sills or shelves, or hung on hooks. A row of wooden, wicker or canvas boxes will provide under-bed storage and maintains a unified look.

Display

Remember that not everything needs to be hidden away. While many items will benefit from being

kept out of sight – for practical as well as aesthetic reasons – storage often involves display as well as concealment. A home without evidence of personal tastes and pleasures will look cold and sterile. Also, you will be less inclined to use items if they are stored away. Keep an edited selection of magazines, home decorations and items you need to hand on view.

Glass-fronted cupboards and bookcases will show off your most-valued possessions or collections and keep them orderly and dust-free, too.

Shelving

Shelving is a popular and effective method of combining storage and display. For a minimal style, use 'floating shelves', which have no visible means of support to interfere with their clean lines. Built-in shelving looks tidy, especially in alcoves where the shelves are cut to fit the space. Adjustable shelving systems are flexible and easy to install, and the brackets and fixings are often covered by the contents, although brackets and supports are part of the design in many modern high-tech systems. Using different materials with decorative or unusual brackets can turn a shelf into a feature, and serendipitous finds, such as ornate wall units and old-fashioned plate racks, can add charm and light relief to an otherwise disciplined environment.

Single shelves can be built at high or low level to continue the established lines of the interior. For a cohesive arrangement, display either a small number of carefully chosen objects or small groups of items in similar colours or styles where you can see and appreciate them. Open shelving allows immediate access, and will look organized if items are sorted by category and a full wall is devoted to the shelves. Free-standing units and bookcases can cover unsightly or irregular walls and work well in certain styles, scales or structures of interior. A wall of books has a library feel that is visually pleasing and looks much simpler than assorted bookcases.

floating

built-in

systems

single

free-standing

Floating shelves

Without supports or brackets to detract from their simplicity, floating shelves are elegant and modern. They can be used singly or in rows and can be purchased in a limited range of sizes from large furniture stores or home-decorating shops, ready to install, or can be custom-built by a carpenter.

Floating shelves are usually made from a single thick piece of solid wood or chipboard with drilled holes that slot onto bolts or dowels fixed into the wall. Alternatively, the shelves are formed from several sections of wood – usually veneered, lacquered or ready-to-paint plywood – to form a thicker construction that fits over a batten screwed to the wall.

Despite their lightweight construction, floating shelves can support a lot of weight, depending on the fixings and the structure of the wall. Long screws are usually needed to support shelves for heavy items, such as books, and partition walls need special toggle or anchor metal fixings that open up behind the panel to grip it.

Built-in shelves

Normally fitted into alcoves, built-in shelving makes maximum use of the space. When painted or finished to match the walls, shelves will blend into the structure of the room, rather than stand out as an addition. Installation will require careful measuring, but a professional carpenter can fit shelves to your specifications.

Materials for shelving should be chosen for the function of the shelves and the structure of the walls. To avoid sagging shelves on wide spans with heavy loads, a thicker material will be needed.

Solid wood looks best, even when painted. Softwoods, such as pine, are relatively inexpensive and therefore widely used, but for a more distinctive look, use large slabs of hardwood, such as oak or beech. Consider using a dark stain on thick softwood shelves to emulate the effect of hardwood. Laminated chipboards are inexpensive, but the edges are vulnerable to damage and the shelves may look less than perfect after a couple of years.

floating shelves

Fixtures will depend on the width of the span. For short spans, shelves can be fixed onto battens attached to the side walls, but for long spans, battens on all three sides may be required. Battens need to be cut shorter than the depth of the shelf and the corners cut away to keep them concealed. Alternatively, a 'lipping' can be fixed across the front of the shelf to disguise the batten, as well as to add thickness to the shelf.

If the shelves are placed high up or far apart, the battens may still be visible. Painting them to blend with the wall will minimize their impact. Slim, metal brackets, which fix to the side walls so that only a narrow right-angle of metal is seen, are also available.

Shelving systems

Modern, elegant shelving systems can be found in a range of materials and prices. Some have glass shelves and slender metal supports that look clean and minimal, whereas others appear industrial and high-tech. They look effective when covering a wall or in a narrow floor-to-ceiling column.

Utility metal shelving systems, used in shops and warehouses and sold by catering suppliers, are now widely available for domestic use. The most common form have mesh shelves that fit together with tubular uprights. They can be bought in sections, with a choice of shelf widths and depths, and adapted to fit any space. Their functional look, large scale and shiny finish make an impact. Other catering units in stainless steel can also be sourced.

Galvanized shelving systems, available from industrial suppliers, have adjustable shelves with angled steel uprights and can be ordered in any length or size.

Luxury, upmarket shelving systems are sophisticated and expensive, but highly versatile. They can be attached to the wall or supported on uprights between

long, low shelving

custom-built window bench

picture shelf

the floor and ceiling. They work well as room dividers, and the variety of components, including desk shelves and cabinets, enable them to be used in work spaces or kitchens.

Inexpensive self-assembly systems can also be used successfully. Some have metal brackets that slot into metal strips fixed to the wall. They are easy to install and effective in a recess, where the shelves can be cut to the same width and depth to give a built-in look. Many have the advantage of being adjustable, in order to accommodate different or changing groups of objects. Though superseded by more sophisticated systems, they do have an honest simplicity that can work well in a pared-down interior.

Single shelves

A single shelf can be both functional and decorative – a

simple way of providing extra storage or an opportunity to display a collection of objects. For storage purposes, a long, single shelf will look more effective than tiers of shorter ones. In a kitchen, a long shelf is useful for providing easy access to frequently used china, glassware, pots and pans. Long, low, wide shelving can provide seating or display, with areas underneath for storage. Alternatively, shelves can run the length of a wall to provide additional work space in a kitchen or office.

On an otherwise bare wall, a single shelf can become a focal point, and a floating version will look particularly modern and understated. In a simple setting, a decorative shelf unit – perhaps an antique market find – can look charming and unexpected. A slab of slate or other unusual material supported on ornate brackets also adds character.

Install a picture shelf to provide a place for displaying photographs, plates or other objects. A narrow wood or metal shelf is ideal for an eye-level collection, which can be changed frequently. A slender strip of aluminium can also be set into a plastered wall, as seen above. If you are using a narrow shelf, make sure it is wide enough to prop objects at a safe angle and that the shelf has a small lip to keep the items in place.

Free-standing units

Inexpensive free-standing shelves and bookcases are available in a range of styles and materials. Choose white or pale wood finishes, or repaint them, if necessary. Wooden shelving systems, where the uprights and shelves are bought separately, do not have to be fixed to the wall. Although rather basic in design, they will be less noticeable if painted to blend in with the walls.

Furnishings

There are no rules when it comes to simple style furnishings. The emphasis is on using furniture carefully and sparingly, disposing of unnecessary items or disguising unattractive ones, or replacing with more streamlined versions. All styles of furniture can be incorporated, from the pared-down lines of contemporary design to the charming and characterful look of old pieces. Neither is it compulsory to keep to one style; the modern approach is an eclectic one, where combinations of old and modern, traditional and ethnic, plain and decorative, cheap and expensive, can work together. The traditional boundaries between cooking, eating, relaxing and working have now virtually disappeared and furniture and furnishings may need to be multifunctional. Tables work well as desks, sofas may be turned into beds and large cupboards can house computers. Your lifestyle and personal taste will, of course, influence your choice of furnishings but comfort should not be sacrificed for style and look.

blending

choosing

renovation

Blending styles

The key to creating a simple look is to blend furnishings by choosing sympathetic materials, colours, shapes and textures. A sleek modern sofa, a battered old box and an ethnic stool will happily coexist in the same room. Hard-edged modern can rub shoulders with faux fur, and antiques can harmonize with chain-store chairs and designer lamps. The exuberant shapes and colours of retro styles often mix well with high-street bargains, and the decorative excesses of period pieces will be tempered by placing them in isolation within a calm, monochrome environment.

Contrasting styles work well and sit comfortably together when the surroundings are understated or when pieces are linked by similar colours, shapes or fabrics. For example, a disparate group of chairs can be unified by painting all the chairs white, but the chairs will also work together if they are of the same wood, or covered in similar types of fabric.

Design classics by le Corbusier, Marcel Breuer, Charles and Ray Eames, and Arne Jacobsen, among many others, are now fully appreciated for their clean lines,

beautiful curves and imaginative use of materials. Many of their designs are still being produced, but the originals are much sought after and may be sourced in outlets specializing in retro pieces. Other quirky pieces from the past, often at relatively low prices, can also be found at these retailers.

Contemporary designs in good-quality materials have recently become more available. The expanding interest in modern furniture has resulted in shops selling bigger ranges by new and established designers. However, the availability of good modern design is no longer confined to upmarket interiors shops; most large furniture companies stock contemporary ranges at mid-price, while other retailers specialize in selling well-designed furniture and home accessories at low cost.

Antique and second-hand
furniture can be found in good condition at house sales, antique markets and fairs, both nationally and abroad. Beautiful antiques or old furniture with a timeless quality will fit in with any style. Simple utilitarian pieces have character and are generally inexpensive. Shops and yards specializing in

antique iron bedstead

house clearance often have good-quality plain furniture that cannot be readily identified as belonging to any special era, but will have an honest charm of its own, and may simply require a coat of paint. If you have spotted a trend that hasn't yet reached the specialist shops, you may be able to get in early with some great bargains. Look for country-style pieces, such as metal bed frames, simple tables and small cupboards.

Ethnic furniture can work well with a simple interior, where it may be fully appreciated against a plain background or as part of a small collection. The increase in foreign travel has exposed us to a wide spectrum of styles and products from other cultures. Travelling abroad is not necessary; plenty of high street shops sell ethnic pieces from such places as Africa, India and the Far East. Specialist shops and dealers are a good source for more unusual or sophisticated examples.

Choosing furnishings

Keeping it simple means fewer pieces of furniture; ideally, everything should earn its place by being beautiful, comfortable and functional. Although it is not always possible for all these criteria to be met – for cost, practical or sentimental reasons – they can help when choosing new furnishings or deciding which ones to eliminate. Any beautiful piece will usually fit in, though if it is distinctive or decorative, you may need to restrain other elements in order to allow it to stand out.

Useful furniture to own includes storage cupboards, bookcases, cabinets with glass doors for display, sofas that double up as beds, tables that can be used as desks, and chests that can also serve as seats or coffee tables.

Scale is an important consideration with furniture, not only for the practical reasons of whether a

piece will fit the available space, but also whether it works with the proportions of the room and the rest of the contents. A simple interior will highlight any discrepancies, but a piece of furniture that may have been considered too big or dominant in a cluttered environment can look perfect in a pared-down setting.

Basic materials used in the construction of furniture have widened in scope. More adventurous and unusual materials, such as plastics, glass, galvanized metal and stainless steel, are now available, in addition to traditional wood and leather.

To create a simple style of interior, you will need to limit the number of elements used, but don't be too disciplined or else your scheme will lack personality. Polished wood, dull metal and the weathered and worn surfaces of old leather and paintwork are mellow and characterful; pale woods, shiny metal or aluminium and the lacquered or plastic finishes of new furniture look cool and sharp.

Upholstery in modern styles is chic, minimal and often makes a bold statement. When buying upholstered furniture, choose neutral colours – they look sophisticated, will blend readily with other pieces of furniture and can be easily incorporated into new decorating schemes when you want a change. Alternatively, a bold sofa, daybed or *chaise longue* can become a centrepiece and provide the basis for the interior design and colour scheme of the room.

neutral modern daybed

No matter how wonderful chairs and sofas may look, they should be comfortable too. When buying upholstered sofas or chairs, try them out in the shop to make sure you can sit or lie in a relaxed position. If you have a piece that is blissfully comfortable, but not attractive, cover it in a neutral fabric and add beautiful cushions and throws to further disguise it, if necessary (see page 121).

Colours should be used in a controlled way for a simple style approach. To harmonize your furnishings with their surroundings, keep to a basic palette. Groups of naturals and neutrals, from pale greys to strong browns, always work well together and will benefit from the addition of textures. Alternatively, use a base of neutrals, but add one or two strong colours as accents. White may seem a good choice for a minimal look, but it stains easily.

Renovation

Old furniture, including antiques, junk-shop finds and pieces you may have had for years, will benefit from regular cleaning, repairing and restoring. Simple care and maintenance can give furniture a new lease of life. For serious renovation, there are specialist books and products on the market, but if you have valuable pieces, seek expert advice.

When renovating old furniture, be careful not to destroy its whole 'character' through over-enthusiastic cleaning. Evidence of age and use is often attractive.

Natural wood will respond well to cleaning, oiling and polishing. Use a mild detergent and water to remove dirt and old wax, and reveal the grain and original colour. Though the result may look pale and dry, feeding the wood with fresh oil and wax, or even a little stain, will enhance it.

furnishings

painted new table

old leather armchair

Metal frames or legs on retro-style furniture can also be scrubbed clean, but don't rub too hard on painted metal or you will damage the finish. Scrubbing old metal that has been painted can often give an attractive 'distressed' finish. To reveal the stark simplicity of bare metal, you will need to strip off all paint, using a proprietary paint stripper if necessary, and rub down the surface with a wire brush or wire wool. A coat of sealant needs to be applied to the metal to avoid rust forming.

Paintwork in good condition simply needs cleaning with a mild detergent and water, but painting or repainting a piece of furniture is a good way to give a fresh, new look. add character or blend a piece into the background.

Sometimes inexpensive furniture is well designed and attractive, but the colour or quality of the material is incompatible with your interior. If

this is the case, consider painting it. Use plain eggshell or gloss paint. A liberal application of white gloss paint can transform a plain but solid table into a stylish object (see page 155).

For a pristine finish on raw wood, first use a primer to provide an even base and prevent paint from soaking in. A fashionably 'distressed' look can be created by painting directly onto the wood with a thin layer of emulsion paint. When dry, rub down with fine-grade sandpaper to reveal some of the wood beneath. Build up several thin layers, rubbing down between each one, and seal with a coat of wax or varnish.

For a smooth finish on metal, first rub it down well to give an even surface, before painting with a primer and enamel paints specified for use on metal.

Old leather has a wonderful mellow quality and an old leather

chair, even a very battered one, adds warmth and character to a room. Leather needs special care. Central heating will dry it out, and old leather will need to be revived and 'fed' to keep it supple and prevent cracking. There are various treatments available for feeding leather, but avoid any oily product on chairs as it may subsequently damage clothes. Saddle soap is a traditional treatment, and very dry leather may require several initial applications and regular treatments thereafter.

Upholstery can be cleaned using one of the many proprietary upholstery cleaners on the market, but there are also professional companies who will do the job quickly and thoroughly. If the upholstery is very worn, it will need to be replaced. Although you can do this yourself, using the services of a professional upholsterer gives the best result.

Loose covers

New covers will transform even the dullest of furniture. As fabrics play an important role in creating the right look, the effect can be quite dramatic. Fitted or tailored covers involve accurate measuring, sewing and securing. Loose covers, however, are easier to make and suit a more relaxed feel.

Choose plain or textured fabrics in solid colours, or, to add interest, simple stripes and patterned prints. Neutral covers can be used to smarten up a tired old sofa or lessen the impact of a large or unattractive one. Choosing a selection of fabrics in a similar type, colour or tone for a group of chairs and sofas will unify them without looking too considered. Unexpected contrasts work well, such as using monogrammed antique linens to cover retro pieces or soften the shape of a modern piece. Covering a traditional sofa in an unexpected material, such as denim, will give it an up-to-date identity (see pages 152–3).

Casual-fit loose covers are easy to make, as they do not have to be a perfect fit. They work well on fully upholstered armchairs and sofas. Simplest of all is a large throw, but unless it is of a substantial material, it can look untidy as soon as anyone sits down.

Tie-on covers are perfect for dining chairs and armchairs without solid arms, but can be used on any style of furniture. Furniture shape will influence the style of the cover, but tie-ons can usually be made with straight seams and flaps rather than complicated constructions.

loose fitted covers

tie-on covers

simple cushions

Accessories

Finishing touches bring colour, texture and a touch of luxury and extravagance to restrained interiors. A mix of textures can be built up using layers of fabrics in complementary tones, and mixing plains with prints or antique linens with lace can look charming.

Cushions knitted in soft wools, such as cashmere, and in both chunky and fine knits, are warm and tactile. Faux fur, suede and velvet add luxury and comfort to a hard-edged interior. Felted wool, flannel and woven tweeds look tailored and smart. White cotton or linen gives a fresh appearance. Use cushions sparingly – a large cushion looks much more chic than a scattering of smaller ones.

Throws, blankets and quilts introduce softness and warmth to a minimal interior, and add a decorative element. They can be draped over armchairs, sofas or beds. Look for faux fur and quilted throws, and those with a contrasting lining or edging. Velvet, cashmere and wool throws drape well and can also be used as comforting wraps in chilly weather. Cream wool blankets with blanket-stitched edges and stripes or windowpane checks look suitably simple. Antique quilts, whether newly purchased or treasured heirlooms, are usually beautifully sewn and have a timeless quality and new quilts are often made in rich velvets, silks and satins.

Bedlinens in white cotton or linen always look fresh and inviting, and pale beiges and greys are more sophisticated. In a pared-down bedroom, brightly coloured linen is cheerful, especially on children's beds. Ginghams and floral prints work especially well when used only for pillowcases, a valance or as a bottom sheet.

Antique linens have a special hand-made quality that makes them soft, subtle and wonderful to sleep on. They wash and bleach well, and there are coarse or fine versions. Old linen sheets made into curtains will hang beautifully; made into loose covers, they give a fresh but relaxed look.

Pictures

Pictures reflect your passions and preferences, and photographs provide evidence of your life and loves. They can be propped against the wall or floor, or on a mantelpiece or shelf. If you intend to display lots of pictures, keep the interior relatively disciplined. The frames or subject matter should be consistent. Simple frames blend, but an ornate or unusual frame provides a focus. One or two large pictures can look dramatic if the colours are bold, but the effect can be subtle and restful when colours harmonize.

Accessories

EGG

36 Kinnerton Street

London SW1X 8ES

tel 020 7235 9315

simple handmade ceramics

EVER TRADING

12 Martindale

London SW14 7AL

tel 020 8878 4050

faux fur throws and cushions

MINT

70 Wigmore Street,

London W1U 2SF

tel 020 7224 4406

*eclectic modern furniture, ceramics
and accessories*

PAPERCHASE

213 Tottenham Court Road

London W1T 9PS

tel 020 7467 6200

Japanese papers and stationery

SUMMERILL AND BISHOP

100 Portland Road

London W11 4LN

tel 020 7221 4566

*French and Italian cookware
and cutlery*

TOAST

tel 01558 668 800 for mail order

www.toastbypost.co.uk

Bedlinens, blankets and quilts

THE WHITE COMPANY

Unit 30

Perivale Industrial Park

Horthendon Lane South

Greenford

Middlesex UB6 7RJ

tel 08701 601610

*Bedlinens, blankets, towels
and quilts*

Antiques/Retro Furniture

AFTER NOAH

121 Upper Street

London N1 1QP

tel 020 7359 4281

www.afternoah.com

DAVID WAINWRIGHT

61-63 Portobello Road

London W11 3DB

tel 020 7727 0707

DECORATIVE LIVING

55 New Kings Road

London SW6 4FE

tel 020 7736 5623

*good simple selection of
English, French and some
ethnic furniture*

JOSEPHINE RYAN

63 Abbeville Road

London SW4 9JW

tel 020 8675 3900

*plain and decorative country
antiques, particularly
white-painted*

JUDY GREENWOOD

659 Fulham Road

London SW6 5PY

tel 020 7736 6037

antique French beds and furniture

THE LACQUER CHEST

72 Kensington Church Street

London W8 4BG

tel 020 7937 1306

fax 020 7376 0223

OVERDOSE ON DESIGN

182 Brick Lane

London E1 6SA

tel 020 7613 1266

*mid-century classics and
modern furniture*

PHILIPS AUCTIONEERS

101 New Bond Street

London W1S 1SR

tel 020 7629 6602

fax 020 7629 8876

www.philips-auctions.com

sale rooms nationwide

PIMPERNEL ANTIQUES

596 Kings Road

London SW6 2DX

tel 020 7731 2448

restored antique upholstery

SOURCE

93–95 Walcot Street

Bath

Avon BA1 3SD

tel 01225 469200

fax 01255 832800

original retro kitchens

TWENTIETH CENTURY DESIGN LTD

274 Upper Street

London N1 2UA

tel 020 7288 1996

Architectural Salvage and Reclamation

ARCHITECTURAL SALVAGE

www.salvoweb.com

*website for specialists in
architectural salvage and reclaimed
building materials*

LASSCO

Clergy House

Mark Street

London EC2A 4ER

tel 020 7749 9944

architectural salvage

WALCOT RECLAMATION LTD

108 Walcot Street

Bath

Avon BA1 5BG

tel 01225 444404

Bathrooms

ASTON MATTHEWS
141 Essex Road
London N1 2SN
tel 020 7226 3657
Extensive range of modern and
traditional bathrooms

AVANTE GLASS BATHROOM PRODUCTS
Unit 2 Dragon Court
Springwell Road
Leeds LS12 1EY
tel 01132 445337
fax 01132 427941
www.avante-bathroom-products.co.uk
bathroom fixtures, basins, etc.

C P HART
212 Arch
Hercules Road
London SE1
tel 020 7902 1000
www.cphart.co.uk
wide range of kitchen and
bathroom furniture and fittings
Showrooms in London, Guildford,
Manchester and Glasgow

DURAT
Durat design by Tonester Ltd, Finland
www.durat.com
stone-like moulded composite for
sinks, baths and basins

IDEAL STANDARD
The Bathroom Works
National Avenue
Kingston Upon Hull HU5 4HS
tel 01482 346461
fax 01482 445886
www.ukcustomercare@aseur.com
bathroom fittings, including special
range to fit in small spaces

THE WATER MONOPOLY
16–18 Lonsdale Road
London NW6 6RD
tel 020 7624 2636
fax 020 7624 2631
French and English antique and
reproduction sanitaryware

Fabrics

DESIGNERS GUILD
275–277 Kings Road
London SW3 5EN
tel 020 7351 5775
plain and textured cotton and wool
fabrics, contemporary patterns, as
well as wallpaper, modern furniture,
upholstery and accessories

LENA PROUDLOCK
tel 01666 890230 for mail order
coloured denim

THE NATURAL FABRIC COMPANY
Wessex Place
127 High Street
Hungerford
Berkshire RG17 0DL
tel 01488 684 002
plain linens, cotton weaves
and ticking

NEISHA CROSLAND
137 Fulham Road
London SW3 6SD
tel 020 7589 4866
modern printed fabrics and
wallpapers

RUSSELL AND CHAPPLE
68 Dury Lane
London WC2B 5SP
tel 020 7836 7521
cotton canvas and linen

WHALEY'S LTD
Harris Court
Great Horton
Bradford
Yorkshire BD7 4EQ
tel 01274 576718
natural and bleached cottons, silks
and linens

ZIMMER AND RHODE
15 Chelsea Harbour Design Centre
London SW10 0XE
tel 020 7351 7115
contemporary wool, linen, cotton
and viole fabrics

Floors

CRUCIAL TRADING
PO Box 11
Duke Place
Kidderminster
Worcs DY10 2JR
tel 01562 820006
fax 01562 820030
e-mail sales@crucial-trading.com
www.crucial-trading.com
natural floor coverings, including
coir, sisal, seagrass, jute, wool
and marmoleum

DALSOUPLE
PO Box 140
Bridgwater
Somerset TA5 1HT
tel 01984 667233
fax 01984 667 366
e-mail info@dalsouple.com
www.dalsouple.com
rubber flooring, also suitable for
work surfaces

FIRED EARTH
Twyford Mill
Oxford Road
Adderbury
Oxon OX17 3HP
tel 01295 812088
fax 01295 810832
www.firedearth.co.uk
wooden and stone flooring,tiles,
paints, natural floor coverings
and rugs

FORBO
Forbo Ireland Ltd
2 Deansgrange Business Park
Blackrock
Co Dublin
tel 01 2898 898
fax 01 2898 177
e-mail info@forb-irl.com
marmoleum flooring

HARDWOOD FLOORING COMPANY
146 West End Lane
London NW6 1SD
tel 020 7328 8481
range of natural woods

JOHNSON
H & R Johnson Tiles Limited
Highgate Tile Works
Tunstall
Stoke-on-Trent ST6 4JX
tel 01782 575 575
fax 01782 577377
www.johnson-tiles.com
ceramic tiles for floors and walls
(available worldwide)

LITHOFIN
tel 01962 732126 for stockists
e-mail sales@lithofin.co.uk
products for treatment, protection
and cleaning of ceramic tiles,
stone and artificial stone floors

ROGER OATES DESIGN
1 Munro Terrace
Cheyne Walk
London SW10 0DL
tel 020 7351 2288
fax 020 7351 6841
e-mail london@rogeroates.com
www.rogeroates.com
natural floorcoverings and fabrics

SOLID FLOOR
53 Pembridge Road
Notting Hill
London W11 3HG

tel 020 7221 9166
fax 020 7221 8193
www.solidfloor.co.uk
wooden flooring

Also at:
128 St John Street
London EC1V 4JS
tel 020 7251 2917
fax 020 7253 7419

Binks Building
30–32 Thomas Street
Northern Quarter
Manchester M4 1ER
tel 0161 8326369
fax 0161 8326372

STONE AGE
19 Filmer Road
London SW6 7BU
tel 020 7385 7954/5
fax 020 7385 7956
www.estone.co.uk
natural stone flooring and work surfaces

Also at:
14 Kings Road
Bristol BS8 4AB
tel 01179 238180
fax 01179 238187

STONELL
Head office
Forstal House
Beltring
Paddock Wood
Kent TN 12 6PY
tel 01235 861566
fax 01892 833600
e-mail admin@stonell.co.uk
www.stonell.com
natural stone flooring, work surfaces, sinks, etc.

Also in:
London, Amersham, Cambridge, Cheltenham, Guildford and Wantage

Heating

BISQUE
244 Belsize Road
London NW6 4BT
tel 020 7328 2225
fax 020 7328 9845
www.bisque.co.uk
radiators

Also at:
15 Kingsmead Square
Bath BA1 2AE
tel 01225 469244
fax 01225 444708

CLYDE COMBUSTIONS LIMITED
Cox Lane
Chessington
Surrey KT9 1SL
tel 020 8391 2020
fax 020 8397 4598
e-mail info@clydecomb.com
fireplaces and traditional-style radiators

CVO FIREVAULT
36 Great Titchfield Street
London W1W 8BQ
tel 020 7580 5333
www.cvo.co.uk
modern gas fires

THE EDWARDIAN FIREPLACE COMPANY
1A Stile Hall Parade
Chiswick High Road
London W4 3AG
tel 020 8995 2554
www.edwardianfires.com
traditional, period and contemporary fireplaces

Also in:
Dulwich and Wandsworth

THE FLOOR WARMING COMPANY
DK Heating Systems UK Ltd
Marlborough House
159 High Road
Wealdstone
Middlesex HA3 5DX
tel 020 8861 2844
fax 020 8861 2414
e-mail dkheating.uk@virgin.net
www.dkheating.com
underfloor heating

HUDEVAD
Bridge House
Bridge Street
Walton-on-Thames
Surrey KT12 1AL
tel 01932 247835
fax 01932 247694
e-mail sales@hudevad.co.uk
www.hudevad.co.uk
radiators

THE PLATONIC FIREPLACE COMPANY
Phoenix Wharf
Eel Pie Island
Twickenham
Middlesex TW1 3DY
tel/fax 020 8891 5904
www.platonicfireplaces.co.uk
modern gas fires

RADIATING STYLE
Unit 15
Derby Road Industrial Estate
Derby Road
Hounslow
Middlesex TW3 3UQ
e-mail sales@radiating style.co.uk
www.radiatingstyle.co.uk
radiators

SPRINZ
Bath and GlassWorks Ltd
137 Western Road
Hurstpierpoint
West Sussex BN6 9SZ

tel 01273 831846

fax 01273 831847

e-mail sales@bathandglass.com

www.bathandglass.com

glass radiators

Kitchens

AGA COOKERS

tel 0845 7125207 for brochure

ALNO (UK) LTD

Unit 10

Hampton Farm Industrial Estate

Hampton Road

West Hanworth

Middlesex TW13 6DB

tel 020 8898 4781

www.alno.co.uk

AMERICAN APPLIANCES

17–19 Mill Lane

Woodford Green

Essex IG8 OUN

tel 0208 506 6600

www.usaappliances.com

Also at:

34a Haddington Place

Edinburgh EH7 4AG

tel 01315 587111

BULTHAUP KITCHENS

37 Wigmore Steet

London W1U 1PP

tel 020 7495 3663

fax 020 7495 0139

www.bulthaup.com

CRABTREE KITCHENS

The Sorting Office

17 Station Road

Barnes

London SW13 0LF

tel 020 8392 6955

e-mail design@crabtreekitchens.
co.uk

www.crabtreekitchens.co.uk

Also at:

The Twickenham Centre

Norcutt Road

Twickenham

Middlesex TW2 6SR

tel 020 8755 1121

Bristol 01179 292293

Dumfriesshire 01387 740288

HABITAT

tel 08456 010740 for branches
nationwide and worldwide

e-mail customerrelations@
habitat.co.uk

www.habitat.net

*modern furniture, lighting, fabrics,
rugs, kitchens, etc.*

IKEA UK LTD

tel 020 8208 5600

www.ikea.com

*modern furniture, kitchens,
lighting, fabrics,accessories, etc.*

LACANCHE

Fourneaux de France Ltd

30 Albion Close

Newtown Business Park

Poole

Dorset BH12 3LL

tel 01202 733011 for brochure

fax 01202 733499

www.lacanche.co.uk

range cookers from France

PAGES

121 Shaftesbury Avenue

London WC2

tel 020 7379 6334

professional kitchen equipment

PLAIN AND SIMPLE KITCHENS

1 Filmer Studios

75 Filmer Road

London SW6 7JF

tel 020 7731 2530

www.plainandsimplekitchens.com

ROUNDHOUSE DESIGN

25 Chalk Farm Road

London NW1 8AG

tel 020 7428 9955 for information
and brochure

e-mail info@roundhousedesign.
com

www.roundhousedesign.com

kitchens and furniture

Also at:

857 Fulham Road

London SW6 5HJ

tel 020 7736 7362

Worcestershire 01684 567323

SIEMATIC UK

Osprey House

Rookery Court

Primett Road

Stevenage

Herts SG1 3EE

tel 01438 749780 for brochure

www.siematic.co.uk

STOVES

tel 01514 308497 for stockists

www.stoves.co.uk

range cookers

Lighting and Furniture

AERO

96 Westbourne Grove

London W2 5RT

tel 020 7221 1950

www.aerofurniture.com

*modern furniture, lighting and
accessories*

ALMA HOME

12–14 Greatorex Street

London E1 5NF

tel 020 7377 0762

fax 020 7375 2471

www.almahome.com

leather furnishings

CATH KIDSTON

8 Clarendon Cross

London W11 4PE

tel 020 7221 4000

plain painted utilitarian furniture

THE CONRAN SHOP

tel 020 7589 7401 for branches

www.conran.com

*modern furniture, lighting, fabrics
and accessories*

Also in:

London, Paris, New York,
Hamburg, Berlin, Dusseldorf,
Tokyo and Fukuoka

DORPLAN ARCHITECTURAL
HARDWARE

434–436 Mutton Lane

Potters Bar

Hertfordshire EN6 3AT

tel 01707 647647

door furniture

GEOFFREY DRAYTON

85 Hampstead Road

London NW1 2PL

tel 020 7387 5840 for store
details

www.geoffrey-drayton.co.uk

modern furniture and accessories

HABITAT

tel 08456 010740 for branches
nationwide and worldwide

e-mail customerrelations@
habitat.co.uk

www.habitat.net

*modern furniture, lighting, fabrics,
rugs, kitchens, etc.*

HEALS

196 Tottenham Court Road

London W1T 7LQ

tel 020 7636 1666 for
store details

www.heals.co.uk

paints
planning
storage
windows

directory

IAN MANKIN
109 Regents Park Road
London NW1 8UR
tel 020 7722 0997 for mail order
natural fabrics

Also at:
271 Wandsworth Bridge Road
London SW6 2TX
tel 020 7371 8825

IKEA UK LTD
tel 020 8208 5600
www.ikea.com
modern furniture, kitchens,
lighting, fabrics, accessories, etc.

INHOUSE
28 Howe Street
Edinburgh
tel 01315 525902
contemporary furniture and
accessories

ISOKON PLUS
Turnham Green Terrace Mews
London W4 1QU
tel 020 8994 0636
fax 020 8994 5635
www.isokonplus.com
classic and contemporary furniture

JERRY'S HOME STORE
163–167 Fulham Road
London SW3 6SN
tel 020 7581 0909
American classic furniture and
accessories

LONDON LIGHTING COMPANY
135 Fulham Road
London SW3 6RT
tel 020 7589 3612
modern lighting

NICE HOUSE
Italian Centre Courtyard
Ingram Street

Glasgow
Scotland G1 1DN
tel 01415 331377

NICOLE FAHRI HOME
17 Clifford Street
London W1X 6SL
tel 020 7494 9051
classic antique furniture and linens,
modern glass and ceramics

PALMA LILAC
tel 020 7912 0882 for
appointment
modern stainless-steel furniture,
Perspex shutters and accessories

PURVES & PURVES
220–224 Tottenham Court Road
London W1T 7QE
tel 020 7580 8223
www.purves.co.uk
modern furniture, lighting and
accessories

SELFRIDGES
Oxford Street
London W1A 1AB
tel 020 7629 1234
good range of modern furniture,
accessories and bedlinens

SCP
135–139 Curtain Road
London EC2A 3BX
tel 020 7739 1869
fax 020 7729 4224
e-mail scp@scp.co.uk
www.scp.co.uk
modern furniture and accessories

SKK
34 Lexington Street
London W1F 0LH
tel 020 7434 4095
e-mail skk@easynet.co.uk
www.skk.net
modern lighting

VIADUCT
1–10 Summers Street
London EC1R 5BD
www.viaduct.com
modern furniture

Paints

ARTHUR SANDERSON & SONS LTD
Sanderson House
Oxford Road
Denham UB9 4DX
tel 01895 830127
www.sanderson-uk.com
paints and wallpapers

DULUX
Dulux Advice Centre
tel 01753 550555 for product
information and stockists
www.dulux.co.uk

FARROW AND BALL
Uddens Estate
Wimborne
Dorset BH21 7NL
tel 01202 876141 for stockists
fax 01202 873793
email info@farrow-ball.com
www.farrow-ball.com
Showrooms in London, Paris
and Toronto

FIRED EARTH
Twyford Mill
Oxford Road
Adderbury
Oxon OX17 3HP
tel 01295 812088
fax 01295 810832
www.firedearth.co.uk
paint ranges by Kelly Hoppen and
Kevin McCloud

NUTSHELL
tel 0136 473801 for mail order
Natural paints, Swedish floor soap
and waxes for wood

PAINT AND PAPER LIBRARY

5 Elystan Street

London SW3 3NT

tel 020 7823 7755

fax 020 7823 7766

www.paintlibrary.co.uk

paints and wallpapers by Neisha
Crosland, Emily Todhunter, David
Oliver and Nina Campbell (paint only)

Also at:

Fonthill Ltd

979 Third Avenue

New York NY 10022

USA

tel 001 212 755 6700

Planning

BCA

Centre for Concrete Information

Century House

Telford Avenue

Crowthorne

Berkshire RG45 6YS

tel 01344 725725

BUILDING CENTRE

26 Store Street

London WC1E 7BT

tel 09065 161136 (calls charged
at £1.50 per minute)

e-mail information@building
centre.co.uk

www.buildingcentre.co.uk

COUNCIL OF REGISTERED GAS

INSTALLERS (CORGI)

tel 08705 168111

www.shop.corgi_gas.com

THE NATIONAL ASSOCIATION OF

CHIMNEY SWEEPS

Unit 15 Emerald Way

Stone Business Park

Stone

Staffordshire ST15 0SR

tel 01785 811732

ROYAL INSTITUTE OF BRITISH

ARCHITECTS (RIBA)

Client Services

66 Portland Place

London W1B 1AD

tel 020 7307 3700

fax 020 7436 9112

e-mail cas@inst.riba.org

www.architecture.com

(Find an Architect)

Storage

BISLEY OFFICE FURNITURE

Queens Road

Bisley

Surrey GU24 9BJ

tel 01483 574577 for stockists

H C SLINGSBY PLC

Unit 8

Della Park

London SW18 1EG

tel 020 8877 0778

metal mesh commercial shelving
systems and other products

THE HOLDING COMPANY

243–245 Kings Road

London SW3 5EL

tel 020 7352 1600

storage specialists

MS STORAGE EQUIPMENT

Park Lane Business Centre

78 Park Lane

Poynton

Cheshire SK12 1RE

tel 01625 858555

fax 01625 858262

www.msstorage.co.uk

lockers

MUJI

tel 020 7494 1197 for stockists
and mail order

modern Japanese storage and
stationery

VITSOE

85 Arlington Avenue

London N1 7BA

tel 020 7354 8444

fax 020 7354 9888

e-mail email@vitsoe.com

www.vitsoe.com

606 Universal Shelving System

Windows

JOHN LEWIS PARTNERSHIP

tel 020 7629 7711 for branches

www.johnlewis.co.uk

wide range of curtain fixtures,
fabrics and ready-made curtains

INFO WORKS

71 Bond Way

London SW8 1SQ

tel 020 7793 0677

fax 020 7793 0122

www.rosso-objekte.com

modern curtain fixing systems

SILENT GLISS

Star Lane

Margate

Kent CT9 4EF

tel 01843 863571

fax 01843 864503

e-mail info@silent-gliss.co.uk

www.silentgliss.co.uk

modern blinds and window
coverings

index

index

I would like express my gratitude to the following people who so willingly allowed us to photograph their homes: Agnes Emery, Alex Sigmon and Alexander Jakowec, Anya van de Wetering, Barbara Davis, Bonnita Postma, Danielle Siden, Ed and Jo Howell, Freeny Yianni, Irene de Coninck, Ischa van Delft, Janie Jackson, Linda Loenen, Nathalie van Reeth, Nicolette le Pelley, Thecla Stuyling de Lange and Tricia Foley.

A big thank you to all at Quadrille, especially Anne Furniss, Mary Evans, Nicky Marshall and Sue Storey, firstly for giving me the opportunity to work on Simple Style and secondly for working together so relentlessly to produce it.

Special thanks to Hotze Eisma for his enthusiasm, good company and of course for taking beautiful photographs with such ease.

I am indebted to Bridget Bodoano for her words, sanity and sense of humour; Lisa Dyer for pulling it altogether at the end with verve and efficiency.

I would also like to thank Esther Jostmeyer and Jo Tyler for their assistance and companionship – making our days so enjoyable. Thanks also to Fiona at Limelight for her support and generally looking after me.

On the home front, I would like to express my gratitude to Becky for looking after my children so well, making it so much easier to work away from home; and of course a huge hug to Gum for holding the fort together, being endlessly supportive and a great dad.

acknowledgments